INTERCOURSE BETWEEN INDIA AND THE WESTERN WORLD

[*Photografisch Atelier, Soerabaia, Java.*

A Hindu ship arriving at Java

(*Borobudur Sculptures*)

Intercourse between India and the Western World

FROM THE EARLIEST TIMES TO
THE FALL OF ROME

H.G. RAWLINSON

MANOHAR
2023

First published 1916
Reprinted 2022, 2023

ISBN 978-93-90035-79-3

Published by
Ajay Kumar Jain *for*
Manohar Publishers & Distributors
4753/23 Ansari Road, Daryaganj
New Delhi 110 002

Printed at
Replika Press Pvt. Ltd.

CONTENTS

I.	From the Earliest Times to the Fall of Babylon	1
II.	The Persian Period. Herodotus: Ktesias	16
III.	The Maurya Empire. Megasthenes	33
IV.	Greek and Semi-Greek Dynasties of the Panjāb	69
V.	The Ptolemies	88
VI.	India and the Roman Empire	101
VII.	India and the Roman Empire (*continued*)	127
VIII.	The Effects of the Intercourse between India and the West	155
	Bibliography	181
	Index	183

ILLUSTRATIONS

A Hindu ship arriving at Java . . . *frontispiece*

Aśoka Pillar (Indo-Persian) . . . . *to face p.* 64

Indo-Greek and Indian Coins (with descriptions) . . . . . *between pp.* 84 *and* 85

Kuvera (from an Indo-Greek sculpture) *to face p.* 154

MAP

India and Central Asia . . . . . *at end*

PREFACE

I HAVE attempted, in this monograph, to furnish a succinct account of the intercourse between India and the Greco-Roman world from the earliest times to the fall of Rome. This subject has never, so far as I am aware, been dealt with as a whole in any English work. Yet it is replete with interest to the student of Hellenism in its wider and more neglected aspects, and to Orientalists, who depend largely upon references in Greek and Roman authors for information about many obscure points of Indian History.

I have, so far as possible, consulted every passage bearing upon India in Roman and Greek Literature. Many, but not quite all, of these passages have been collected, annotated, and translated by the late Dr J. W. McCrindle, in his six valuable volumes of translations of such references. On these the present monograph is very largely based, though I have, in nearly every case, referred to the original text rather than to the translation.

The difficulties of a work of this kind are considerable in India, where up-to-date libraries are few and far between, and the verification of references is proportionately tedious and laborious. I owe, therefore, a special debt of gratitude to Professor E. J. Rapson, who has read through my proofs, made numerous suggestions and corrections, and assisted me in many ways; to Dr P. Giles, Master of Emmanuel College, for criticisms and references; and lastly, to the authorities of the University Press, for their unfailing courtesy and promptitude. The map is reproduced by kind permission of Messrs Longmans, Green and Co.; the coin plate was prepared at the British Museum, under Professor Rapson's directions. The photographs are produced with the permission of the Director General of Archaeology, with the exception of the Javanese plate, which I owe to Mr H. J. Lewis, of the Atelier at Soerabaia.

H. G. RAWLINSON.

POONA, 1916.

CHAPTER I

FROM THE EARLIEST TIMES TO THE FALL OF BABYLON

'Quinquiremes of Nineveh from distant Ophir
Rowing home to haven in sunny Palestine:
With cargoes of ivory, and apes and peacocks,
Sandalwood, cedarwood, and sweet, white wine.'
J. MASEFIELD.

FROM prehistoric times, three great trade-routes have connected India with the West. The easiest, and probably the oldest of these, was the Persian Gulf route, running from the mouth of the Indus to the Euphrates, and up the Euphrates to where the road branches off to Antioch and the Levantine ports. Then there was the overland route, from the Indian passes to Balkh, and from Balkh either by river, down the Oxus to the Caspian, and from the Caspian to the Euxine, or entirely by land, by the caravan road which skirts the Karmanian Desert to the north, passes through the Caspian Gates, and reaches Antioch by way of Ktesiphon and Hekatompylus. Lastly, there is the circuitous sea route, down the Persian and Arabian coasts to Aden, up the Red Sea to Suez, and from Suez to Egypt on the one hand and Tyre and Sidon on the other. It must not be supposed, of course, that merchandise travelled from India to Europe direct. It changed hands at great emporia like Balkh, Aden or Palmyra, and was often, no doubt, bartered many times on the way. This accounts for the vagueness and inaccuracy of the accounts of India which filtered through to the West in early times. A story is always vastly changed in passing through many hands.

Trade between the Indus valley and the Euphrates is, no doubt, very ancient. The earliest trace of this intercourse is probably to be found in the cuneiform inscriptions of the Hittite kings of Mitanni in Kappadokia, belonging to the fourteenth or fifteenth century B.C. These kings bore Aryan names, and worshipped the Vedic gods, Indra, Mitra, Varuṇa, and the Aśvins, whom they call by their Vedic title *Nāsatyā*. They were evidently closely connected, though we cannot yet precisely determine how, with the Aryans of the Vedic Age, who were at that time dwelling in the Panjāb[1]. It has been claimed that the word *Sindhu*, found in the library of Assurbanipal (668–626 B.C.), is used in the sense of "Indian cotton," and the word is said to be much older, belonging in reality to the Akkadian tongue, where it is expressed by

[1] These names were discovered by Prof. Hugo Winckler on a cuneiform tablet at the Hittite capital of Boghazköi, in 1907. See Ed. Meyer in vol. 42 of Kuhn's *Zeitschrift*, and the discussions by Oldenburg, Keith, Sayce, and Kennedy in *J.R.A.S.* 1909, pp. 1094–1119.

ideographs meaning "vegetable cloth[1]." Assurbanipal is known to have been a great cultivator, and to have sent for Indian plants, including the "wool-bearing trees" of India. At any rate, we know that the cotton trade of western India is of great antiquity. The Indians, when the Greeks first came into contact with them, were dressed in "wool grown on trees[2]." In the *Ṛig Veda*, Night and Dawn are compared to "two female weavers[3]." We may perhaps trace to this source the Greek σινδών, the Arabic *satīn* (a covering), and the Hebrew *sadīn*[4]. Similarly the Hebrew *karpas* and the Greek κάρπασος come from the Sanskrit *karpāsa*. Logs of Indian teak have been found in the temple of the Moon at Mugheir (the "Ur of the Chaldees") and in the palace of Nebuchadnezzar, both belonging to the sixth century B.C., and we know that the trade in teak, ebony, sandalwood and blackwood, between Barygaza and the Euphrates, was still flourishing in the second century A.D.[5] In the swampy country at the mouth of the Euphrates, nothing but the cypress grows well.

On the obelisk of Shalmaneser III, 860 B.C., are apes, Indian elephants, and Baktrian camels; and

[1] Sayce, *Hibbert Lectures*, 1887, p. 138. Max Müller, *Physical Religion* (1891), p. 25. This has been since doubted, however.

[2] Herod. III. 106.

[3] *Ṛig-Veda*, II. 3. 6.

[4] Mentioned in Isaiah III. 23, among the *foreign luxuries* imported into Judaea. The A.V. translates it "fine linen." Linen and cotton are often confused in ancient literature. Flax, of course, came from Egypt.

[5] *Periplus Maris Erythraei*, § 36.

in one of the *Jātaka* stories, called the *Bāberu Jātaka*[1], we hear of Indian merchants who took periodical voyages to the land of *Bāberu* (Babylon). There were very few birds in that country, and on their first visit the merchants brought with them an Indian crow, which excited great admiration. But on a subsequent voyage they took a wonderful performing peacock, and the poor crow found himself quite eclipsed!

Indians appear in those days to have been experienced sailors. Early Indian literature contains abundant references to ships and sea-faring, and bears testimony to the skill and daring of Hindu mariners in remote times. There are many allusions in the *Ṛig Veda* to voyages by sea[2]. In the longest of these passages, we hear of voyages to distant islands, and galleys with a hundred oars[3]. Evidently from early days the Indian seamen built ships larger than those usually employed even at a much later date in the Mediterranean. In the story of the invasion of Ceylon, probably in the sixth century B.C., by the Bengal prince Vijaya and his followers, we hear of a ship large enough to hold over seven hundred people[4]. This may be an exaggeration, but references to ships holding

[1] Trans. Cowell and Rouse (Cambridge, 1907), III. p. 83. This tale probably dates from the fifth century B.C. Professor Minayef first drew attention to this point.

[2] *e.g.* *Ṛig Veda*, I. 25. 7, 56. 2, 97. 7, 116. 3; II. 48. 3; VII. 88. 3, etc. Bühler, *Origin of the Brāhma Alphabet*, p. 84.

[3] *Ṛig Veda*, I. 116. 3.

[4] *Mahāvaṃsa*. Tr. Turnour, Ch. VI *fin.*

three[1], five[2], and even seven[3] hundred people are to be found in the *Jātaka* stories. Indeed, Buddhist literature in particular abounds in allusions to sea-voyages, and we gather that traders visited Babylon, Ceylon, and the Golden Chersonese (*Suvarṇabhūmi*)[4]. The chief ports were Champa and Tāmralipti on the east coast, and Bharukaccha and Suppāra on the west[5]. The exports in which they dealt were various kinds of birds and beasts, including, curiously enough, the valuable Sind horses[6], ivory, cotton goods, jewels, gold, and silver. Emigration was not uncommon. One of the most interesting of these early references to sea-borne traffic is to be found in the *Kevaddhu Sutta*[7], where we read how *long ago* merchants sailed far out of sight of the coast, taking "shore-sighting" birds, which were released from time to time, in order that they might guide the mariners to land. This custom, which reminds us of the familiar episode of the story of Noah, is mentioned by Pliny[8] and Kosmas Indikopleustes as existing among the Sinhalese.

[1] Cambridge ed. II. 128 (*Vālahassa Jātaka*). [2] *Ibid.*

[3] *Ibid.* IV. 138 (*Suppāraka Jātaka*). For the whole subject, see Mukerji, *Indian Shipping*, Ch. III (Longmans, 1912).

[4] *Mahājanaka Jātaka*, Cambridge ed. VI. 32; *Saṅkha Jātaka*, *ibid.* VI. 15.

[5] See *e.g.* the *Suppāraka Jātaka*, Cambridge ed. IV. 138.

[6] *Kuṇḍaka-Kucchi-Sindava-Jātaka*, Cambridge ed. II. 287 *et passim*.

[7] Rhys Davids, *J.R.A.S.* 1899, p. 432. Probably fifth century B.C. [8] *N.H.* VI. 22.

The Persian Gulf trade was at first principally in the hands of the Chaldaeans, a troublesome nation, given to piracy, but they were exterminated in 694 B.C. by Sennacherib with the aid of a great fleet which he built upon the Tigris. Sennacherib, after breaking up this nest of pirates, sent them to dwell in Gerrha, where the heat was so fierce that they were forced to use blocks of salt to build their houses[1]. The trade of the Persian Gulf then fell into the hands of the ubiquitous Phoenicians, a colony of whom, according to Justin[2], had settled in the Babylonian marshes, having been driven out of their own land by earthquakes. Abundant evidence of the presence of these merchants was visible in the days of Strabo on the Bahrein Islands, at the mouth of the Persian Gulf[3]. These remains have lately been excavated and many interesting relics were recovered[4].

The Bahrein Islands were the port of call where ships took in water before setting sail for India, as the inhospitable Mekrān coast had nothing to offer them. The immense trade with all nations carried on by the Phoenicians may be estimated by studying the remarkable passage in which the prophet Ezekiel[5] prophesies the overthrow of the great city of Tyre in 573 B.C., by

[1] Strabo, *Geog.* XVI. 53. [2] Justin, XVIII. 3. 2.

[3] *Geog.* XVI. 3. 3–5. He says the shores were dotted with Phoenician temples.

[4] They are in the Prince of Wales Museum, Bombay. See the *Report*, Archaeological Survey, 1912–13.

[5] Ch. XXVII *et seq.*

Nebuchadnezzar II. "Tarshish was thy merchant by reason of the multitude of thy riches: with silver, iron, tin and lead, they traded for thy wares. . . . Dan also, and Javan, going to and fro, occupied in thy fairs: bright iron, cassia and calamus were in thy market. . . . And in their wailing they shall take up a lamentation for thee, and lament over thee, saying, 'Who is there like Tyre, like her that is brought to silence in the midst of the sea? When thy wares went forth out of the seas, thou filledst many peoples; thou didst enrich the kings of the earth with the multitude of thy riches and thy merchandise.'" Herodotus refers to the Phoenician ships as "taking to long voyages, loading their ships with Assyrian and Egyptian wares[1]."

In 606 B.C. came the overthrow of the Assyrian empire, and Babylon took the place of Nineveh as queen of western Asia. In the crowded market-places of that great city met the races of the world,—Ionian traders, Jewish captives, Phoenician merchants from distant Tarshish, and Indians from the Panjāb, who came to sell their wares. "At Babylon," says Berosus, "there was a great resort of people of various races (πολὺ πλῆθος ἀνδρῶν ἀλλοεθνῶν), who inhabited Chaldaea and lived in a lawless fashion." We have already referred to the *Jātaka* story of the Indian merchants who went to Babylon. A Babylonian colony may have sprung up on the borders of

[1] Herod. I. 50.

India, for Strabo tells us that the followers of Alexander found at Taxila a marriage-market conducted on the well-known Babylonian principle[1]. The intercourse between India and the Semitic nations was, however, mostly carried on by sea. The journey from the defiles of the Hindu Kush to the Mediterranean ports was long and dangerous: the mountains, the deserts, and the many wild tribes which lay in the path, presented an almost insurmountable barrier. The old story of the invasion of India by Semiramis is, of course, a fable, and emanates from the notorious Ktesias[2]. There is, however, abundant evidence that such a route existed from very early times. An axe-head of white jade, which could only have come from China, has been found in the second city of Troy[3]. "The most ancient part of Indian art," says a recent critic, "belongs to the common endowment of early Asiatic culture which once extended from the Mediterranean to China and as far south as Ceylon, where some of the most archaic motifs survive in the decoration of pottery. To this Mykenaean facies belong all the simpler arts of woodwork, weaving, metalwork, pottery, etc., together with a group of designs including many of a remarkably Mediterranean aspect,

[1] Strabo, *Geog.* XV. I. 61.

[2] McCrindle, *Ancient India*, p. 10, note. The story is told at length in Diodorus Siculus, II. 16–20. Semiramis is probably Sammurammat, wife of Adad-Nirari IV, 810–782 B.C. She never went near India, or, indeed, east of the Tigris valley.

[3] Schliemann, *Ilios*, p. 240.

others more likely originating in western Asia. The wide extension and consistency of this culture throughout Asia in the second millennium B.C., throws important light on ancient trade intercourse at the time when the eastern Mediterranean formed the western boundary of the civilized world[1]." No doubt the caravans travelled from immemorial times to the great emporium of Baktra, where the roads from India, China, and the West converged: there the cargoes were shipped on to rafts and floated down the Oxus to the Caspian, and thence, partly by land and partly by river, to the Euxine. Or else, travelling entirely by land, the merchants followed the great road which still skirts the Karmanian Desert to the north, passes through the Caspian Gates, and crossing the Euphrates at Thapsacus, ends at Antioch and the Levantine ports[2].

The third, and perhaps the most important of the trade-routes between India and the West, was that which ran from the mouth of the Red Sea to India up the Arabian coast. Its importance lies in the fact that it linked India not only to the gold-fields and the fabulously wealthy incense country of southern Arabia and Somaliland, but to Egypt

[1] Coomaraswamy, *Arts and Crafts of India and Ceylon* (Foulis, 1913), p. 40. See also the *Ostasiatische Zeitschrift*, 1914, p. 385 ff. The most remarkable example is that of the deer with four bodies and a single head. This design, found all over India, from the Ajantā Caves to Tanjore, is figured on a Chalcidian vase of the sixth cent. B.C. (Morin Jean, *Dessin des Animaux en Grèce*, fig. 156).

[2] Strabo, II. I. 15.

and Judaea. Through Judaea, Indian goods found another outlet, by way of the adjacent ports of their allies of Tyre and Sidon, to the Mediterranean.

For unknown years the Egyptians had traded in the Red Sea, fetching spices from the "land of Punt," and from Arabia Felix. No doubt from time to time Indian goods were brought in Arabian vessels to the ancient emporium of Aden. But the Egyptians were poor sailors. About the thirteenth century before Christ, however, a great impetus to the Red Sea trade was given, if we may trust the Jewish chroniclers, by the Phoenicians. David, king of Judah, had conquered Edom, and had thrown open to the Jews the valuable ports of Elath and Ezion Geber[1]. He had also formed an alliance with Hiram, king of Tyre. Solomon, on his accession, suggested to Hiram's son the propriety of establishing a Phoenician trading station in the Red Sea, and the Tyrian monarch, nothing loth, equipped a fleet of "ships of Tarshish[2]," at Ezion Geber. The "navy of Tarshish" made a triennial voyage to the East, bringing back with them a vast quantity of gold and silver, ivory, apes, peacocks, and "great plenty of almug trees and precious stones[3]." The port at which they shipped these goods was Ophir, a place famous for its gold, so much so indeed that the expression

[1] The modern Akaba, at the head of the eastern arm of the Red Sea. In Roman times the port was known as Aelana and the gulf as the Sinus Aelaniticus.

[2] *i.e.* sea-going vessels, such as were used for long voyages.

[3] I Kings II. 26, X. 21; II Chronicles IX. 21, and XVII. 18.

"gold of Ophir" became proverbial in Hebrew[1]. At first sight it appears as if the port of Ophir must have been somewhere on the Indian coast. India was famous for its gold. Ophir appears as *Σωφάρα* in the Septuagint, and Sophir is a term applied in Coptic to southern India. Abhīra[2] and Suppāra[3] have also been proposed. Josephus even locates it in the Golden Chersonese[4]! Then again, most of the articles of commerce mentioned in the Jewish annals have names which may be traced to Indian originals. Thus "ivory" is in the Hebrew text *shen habbin*[5], "elephant's teeth," a literal translation of the Sanskrit *ibhadanta*. The "almug" is in Sanskrit and Tamil *valgu*. The word used for "ape" is not the ordinary Hebrew one, but *koph*, obviously the Sanskrit *kapi*. "Peacocks" are *thuki-im*, the Tamil *tokei*. Again, there is the curious resemblance between the *Mahoshadha Jātaka* and the story of the Judgement of Solomon. In the former story, the Buddha, incarnate in a former birth as *vazir* of the Raja of Benares, has to adjudicate between two women, each of whom claims a certain infant. Now one of the women was a

[1] *e.g.* Job XXII. 24, XXVIII. 16, Psalm XLV. 9, Isaiah XIII. 12, in addition to passages already cited.

[2] Lassen, *Ind. Alt.* I. 538.

[3] Benfey, *Indien*, 30, in Ersch and Grüber's *Encyclopaedia*.

[4] *Ant. Jud.* VIII. 2. For a summary and bibliography of the Ophir literature, see Hastings, *Dictionary of the Bible*, s.v. The best authority is Glaser, *Skizze der Geog. Arab.* (1890), II. 353. Ophir is *between Sheba and Havilah*, Gen. X. 29.

[5] *Habbin* is no doubt a corruption of *ibha*.

yakshiṇī, or ghoul, who had stolen the child to devour it. The Buddha ordered one woman to seize the child's head and the other his legs and to pull, and each should keep what they got. The ghoul, of course, assents, but the rightful mother consents to give up her share of the infant, rather than hurt him. To her the Buddha gives the child[1]. This story, however, may have reached India from Babylon at the time of the Captivity (595–538 B.C.). Again, it is unlikely that the Phoenicians, bold sailors as they were, ever accomplished the lengthy voyage from Suez to an Indian port, particularly a South Indian port, in the primitive vessels then in use. It must be remembered that early mariners could not go very far from the coast[2], and the voyager would have to go right up the Arabian and Persian coasts, an enormously long way. It is much more probable that Ophir was an *entrepôt* on the shores of Arabia, where Indian and Phoenician alike brought their wares and bartered them. "Primitive trade," it has been said, "passes from tribe to tribe and port to port." Ophir was probably at the mouth of the Persian Gulf, on the coast of Oman. Hither came for export the gold from the rich fields of

[1] Cambridge ed. VI. 163. The story is part of the *Ummaga Jātaka*. See also Rhys Davids, *Buddhist Birth stories*, Introd. XIV.

[2] Even the Indian mariner with his "shore-sighting" birds, was probably never more than fifty miles from land. The voyages to Babylon, Ceylon, Burma, etc. were all coasting voyages.

southern Arabia which has made Ophir famous. After the death of Solomon, the trade of Ezion Geber gradually declined with the chequered fortunes of the Jewish nation. Jehoshaphat tried to revive it, but his fleet met with disaster[1] outside the port. The Edomites revolted and were repressed with difficulty, though the neighbouring port of Elath was in Jewish hands until its capture by Tiglath-pileser.

The general effect of this intercourse upon any of the countries concerned was not very great. Articles of commerce, bearing their Indian names, reached, as we have already seen, the western world from time to time. Indian ivory became widely known in the Mediterranean at an early date. The Egyptian word *ebu,* like the Italian *ebur,* is clearly the Sanskrit *ibha.* The Greek root ἐλεφαντ-, like the Hebrew word, appears to represent *ibha-danta,* perhaps with the Arabic prefix *el*[2]. If this is so, the word is an interesting hybrid, betraying an Indian origin and Arabian conveyance to Europe. The word is found in Homer, as is also κασσίτερος, the Sanskrit *kastīra.* Tin and ivory reached Greece at an early period from India. The "ape," like the ivory of Solomon, also found its way to Egypt, if the Egyptian *kafu,* like the Hebrew *koph,* comes from *kapi.* Among substances which originally came from Dravidian

[1] I Kings XXII. 48; II Chron. XX. 36.

[2] There is, however, a good deal of doubt about this prefix. Another possible derivation is the Hebrew *eleph,* ox, like the *bos Lucas* of Lucretius.

ports, we may mention rice, which, like ivory, was originally brought to Europe by Arab traders. The Tamil *arisi* become *aruz* in Arabian and ὄρυζα in Greek[1]. Other articles of trade which reached Europe at various dates from Dravidian ports are aloes (Tamil *aghil*, Hebrew *ahal*); cinnamon (Tamil *karppu*, Greek κάρπιον, first mentioned by Ktesias); ginger (Tamil *inchiver*, Greek ζιγγίβερις); pepper (Tamil *pippali*, Greek πέπερι); and the beryl-stone (Tamil and Sanskrit *vaiḍūrya*, Greek βήρυλλος). The presence of the African Baobab (*Adansonia digitata*) in the Tinavelly district has been traced to early traders from Africa[2].

Whether India was affected in the prehistoric period by her contact with her nearer and more powerful neighbours, the Assyrians and Babylonians, is an interesting question. The *Brāhmī*-script, the parent script of India, was borrowed from Semitic sources, probably about the seventh

[1] See, for the history of Rice, Hewitt, *R.S.A. Journal*, 1890, p. 730.

[2] Caldwell, *Dravidian Grammar*, vol. I. Introduction. Ginger, pepper and the beryl do not occur before Pliny. The word "crimson" (Skt. *krimi*, a worm, cf. vermeil) is another example. Practically all these articles are *Dravidian*, it should be noted, either because in early days Dravidians still held the west coast of India as far as Broach, or because many articles of commerce from South India were sent north for export. The Baobab may have come much later, with the African Mohammedans, or with the Portuguese. The latter, both in India and Africa, make a kind of sherbert from the fruit.

century B.C.[1] The influence of Babylonian mythology may perhaps be detected in Hindu literature. The myth of the Fish Incarnation of Vishṇu in the *Śatapatha Brāhmaṇa* is reminiscent of the Babylonian stories of the Flood[2]. Chaldaean astronomy may be responsible for the division of the sky into twenty-four *nakshatras*, and perhaps we may trace to this ultimate source the division of the week into seven days, named after the sun, moon, and five planets. This, however, was apparently borrowed directly from Alexandria by the Indians, as it is only mentioned in the later astronomical works[3]. The relation between the earliest Indian and Babylonian weights and measures is obscure[4]. In architecture, India owed very little to Babylon, though she borrowed certain details of ornamentation, such as the bell-capital and the lion-pillar, indirectly from Assyria through Persia. Babylonian architecture, owing to the lack of good building stone, was never remarkable. "Babylonian temples are massive but shapeless structures of crude brick supported by buttresses[5].'

[1] Bühler, *Indian Studies*, III. 1895. Perhaps, as Bühler says, from the type of writing represented by the Moabite Stone (890 B.C.). But his arguments are not altogether satisfactory.

[2] This legend is as old as the *Atharva Veda*, and is found in the Avesta (Lindner, *Die Iranische Flutsage*, in Roth's *Festgruss*, 2. 13). For a detailed bibliography, see Macdonell's *Vedic Index* (1912), p. 430, note.

[3] Barnett, *Antiquities of India*, ch. VI, note.

[4] The *Manā hiraṇyayā* of *Ṛig Veda*, VIII. 72. 8 may be the Babylonian and Greek μνᾶ.

[5] *Encyc. Brit.* XIth ed. s.v. *Babylonian Art.*

CHAPTER II

THE PERSIAN PERIOD. HERODOTUS: KTESIAS

IN 538 B.C. the last of the great Semitic Empires of western Asia came to an end. Cyrus and his Iranians stormed the walls of Babylon, and the Persian monarch took the title of "Lord of Sumer, Akkad, Babel and the four quarters of the world." His successor, Darius, built up a great kingdom on the foundations thus prepared for him. His farsighted schemes, which gained for him the contemptuous epithet κάπηλος, The Pedlar, from his nobles, included the conquest of the remote Iranian tribes on the east of the Karmanian Desert. Darius, however, did not stop here. The wealth of the nations of the Indus valley had long been known to the Assyrians and Babylonians, and he determined to add this district to his domains. He probably, like Alexander, advanced upon India from Baktra, and reaching the river Indus at the town of Kaspapyrus (perhaps *Kāsyapapura*), "a frontier city of Gandhāra, on the Skythian borderland," says Hekataeus[1], sent an expedition under a Greek mercenary, Skylax of Karyanda, to explore the

[1] *Frag.* 178. It is in the country of Paktyike, adds Herodotus (IV. 44), who twice mis-spells the word as *Kaspatyrus*. It is not to be connected with Kashmīr (*Kāśyapa-mīra*), or,

river down to its mouth, and when he reached the sea, to sail home, examining on the way the coast-line and its chief features. Presumably Skylax had orders to find his way to the Red Sea, and not to return by the shorter Persian Gulf route, with which, probably, the Persians were already perfectly well acquainted. At any rate, he found his way, after an adventurous voyage of two and a half years' duration, to Arsinoe, the modern Suez, already used by the Egyptians for trade with the East[1]. From the time he took, we may infer that Skylax proceeded in a leisurely fashion, probably enquiring his way from port to port and trading as he went. His road must have lain along the old trade route to Ophir, and from Ophir to Aden along the Arabian coast. To Skylax, as far as we know, belongs the double distinction of having been the first Greek to visit

of course, Kābul. Paktyike is the country of the Pakhtū, Pashtū, or Pathāns. The town, which was later celebrated for its spikenard (*Periplus*, § 48), was probably on the Kābul river, which accounts for the fact that the voyagers sailed at first *eastwards*, as Herodotus says. (See Sir Aurel Stein, *Ancient Geography of Kaśmīr* (1889); H. H. Wilson, *Ariana Antiqua*, p. 137; Lassen, *Ind. Alt.* II. 630; Bunbury, *Ancient Geography*, I. 226, note C.)

[1] Herod. IV. 44. The date of the conquest of India by Darius is between 516 B.C. and his death in 486 B.C. In the Behistūn Inscriptions (c. 516 B.C.) only Gandhāra and Paruparaesanna (Paropamisus) are mentioned. Indians are not spoken of till the Persepolis and Naksh-i-Rastam inscriptions. Hence the expedition took place about 510 B.C.

India, and to make the Red Sea voyage. The latter feat was not repeated till the days of Eudoxus, three centuries later. The memoirs of Skylax have unfortunately perished, though they may have been utilized by Herodotus. Darius annexed the Indus valley and made it the twentieth satrapy of the Persian Empire. At that time the alluvial gold fields of Dardistān produced an immense quantity of gold, and the new province paid to the Great King the enormous tribute of 360 talents of gold-dust[1]. They also supplied a light division to the Persian forces. The statement of Herodotus, that the Persian fleet "*frequented* the sea," seems to imply that Darius considerably developed the sea-traffic[2].

The Greeks, long before the annexation of the Panjāb by Persia, appear to have heard, in a dim sort of way, of India. Homer speaks of two races of Ethiopians, the western, or African Ethiopians, and the eastern Ethiopians[3]. The word

[1] Herod. III. 97. 360 talents of gold = 20,736 ℔ = £1,078,272. No wonder the gold was soon worked out! (Cunningham, *Coins of Ancient India*, p. 12 ff.)

[2] Μετὰ δὲ τούτους περιπλώσαντας, Ἴνδους τε κατεστρέψατο Δαρεῖος, καὶ τῇ θαλάσσῃ ταύτῃ ἐχρᾶτο, IV. 44. Darius tried, amongst other things, to re-open the Suez Canal, a project attempted by more than one of the Pharaohs, and afterwards by Ptolemy Philadelphus. Probably this was suggested to him by the report of Skylax on the richness of the Red Sea traffic.

[3] Αἰθίοπας τοὶ διχθὰ δεδίαται, ἔσχατοι ἀνδρῶν,
οἱ μὲν δυσομένου Ὑπερίονος, οἱ δ' ἀνίοντος. *Od.* I. 23.

Ethiopian is applied by Herodotus to the dark Dravidians of southern India[1], and probably even in the Homeric age it was thought that Asia and Africa united so as to enclose the Indian Ocean like the Mediterranean[2]. In that case there would be no incongruity in applying the word Ethiopian to the dark peoples of India and Africa alike. Even in those early days, Indian goods reached Europe, as the words ἐλέφας, κασσίτερος, and σινδών testify. The first writer, however, to mention India is the father of Greek geography, Hekataeus of Miletus, a contemporary of Skylax[3]. In the fragments of his lost work, the *Periegesis*, eight Indian names occur—the Indus, the Indi, the city of Kaspapyrus, the country of the Gandarii, the Opiae and the Kalliatiae[4], the Skiapodes[5], and the city of Aragante. From his mention of

[1] Herod. VII. 70. Ktesias also calls the Indians Ethiopians. Even the late *Barlaam and Josaphat*, 8th cent. A.D. is actually described in the Preface as coming ἐκ τῆς ἐνδοτέρας τῶν Αἰθιόπων χώρας, τῆς Ἴνδων λεγομένης!

[2] Alexander thought the Indus was the Nile, and the idea of Africa joining Asia was entertained by Ptolemy. On the other hand the fact that many voyagers attempted the circumnavigation of Africa points to the fact that the belief was not universally held. The word "Aethiopian" is really applied to Abyssinia (*Itiopyavan*), perhaps from *Atyōb*, incense.

[3] Fl. c. 520 B.C. Expedition of Skylax to the Red Sea, c. 512–510 B.C.

[4] Kaliantiae in Herodotus. They are not identified.

[5] A fabulous race, who lived, however, in *Libya*, according to Ktesias. Here again India and Africa are confused.

Kaspapyrus, we may conclude that Hekataeus came to know of India through the narrative of Skylax. It is interesting to notice that the Greeks talked of the "Indus" and "Indians," whereas the inhabitants of the country itself spoke of "Sindhu," "Sindhava." Later travellers noticed this with surprise. "Indus incolis *Sindus* appellatus est," says Pliny, and the author of the *Periplus* says that the river is locally called *Sinthus*. The Persians softened the initial *s*, *more suo*, to *h* (the Avesta word is *Hindu*) ; the Ionians, having no aspirate, made the word into "Ἴνδος[1]." The word reached Greece through Persia. In the same way, the Oriental nations heard chiefly of the Greeks through the Ionian traders who had colonized the coasts of Asia Minor. The word for Greek in Hebrew[2] and Sanskrit is *Yavana*, and *Yaunā* in old Persian. This must date from a time when the digamma was still in use. It is a literal transcript of Ἰάϝων. *Yona*, the Prakrit word, is not, of course, derived from *Yavana*, but it is a separate rendering of Ἴων[3].

[1] Thus "India" is Greek, "Hindu" is Persian.

[2] *e.g.* Ezekiel XXVII. 18, Isaiah LXXI. 19, etc. The Jews identified the Javan of Genesis X. 2 with the Ionians. So Milton (*P.L.* 508) :

"Ionian gods of Javan's issue held."

[3] The digamma, however, was lost as early as 800 B.C. Hence it is possible that both *Yavana* and *Yona* are derived from the old Persian *Yaunā*. Probably the Indians heard first of the Ionians through the Persians.

Herodotus, the first Greek writer about India whose account has survived, was born in 484 B.C., at Halikarnassus, not far from Karyanda, the home of Skylax, to whom he may owe not a little of his knowledge. He tells us[1] that the Indians are the last of all the nations on the eastern side of the world; for beyond the Panjāb lay the limitless Rājputāna desert, the *Marusthālī*, or place of death, stretching, as Herodotus thought, to the end of the world. Indians, he says, are of many nations, each speaking a different tongue. He divides them, however, into two broad classes, the dark, barbarous nomads, living in the marshes, and the paler, refined Aryans of the Kaspapura and Pakhtū districts of northern India, whom he appropriately compares to their Iranian kinsmen of Baktria[2]. Besides these, he adds, there are other Indians in the far south, out of the sphere of Persian influence, who resemble the Ethiopians. These are plainly the Dravidian peoples. The aborigines were in his opinion degraded savages. Those of the marshes of the Indus wore clothes made of rushes, lived (like their neighbours, the famous Ichthyophagi of the Mekrān) on raw

[1] The following information is taken from Bk III. 97–106. The voyage of Skylax is mentioned in Bk IV. ch. 44.

[2] Herod. III. 102. Arrian (*Indika*, VI) contrasts the swarthy Dravidians (whom he compares to the Ethiopians) with the fair Aryans "who are white like the Egyptians." Ktesias saw two Indian men and five women "as fair as any in the world" (*Frag.* I. § 9. McCrindle). Many Pathans to-day are as fair as an Englishman.

fish[1], and made rude boats out of a single joint of the gigantic reeds growing near the river[2]. A neighbouring tribe, the Padaei, (who may be the Bhīl and other aboriginal races of central India, where such practices were common till quite recent times[3]), even killed and ate their sick relatives. This disgusting custom, which originates in a religious superstition, was also carried on by certain Skythian tribes[4]. Herodotus also makes a very interesting reference to a religious sect who killed nothing that had life, lived on a grain like millet, and had no houses. It is impossible to help wondering whether we have not here a reference to the Buddhists. Gautama, it will be remembered,

[1] Dried fish still forms a staple food for Indians on the coasts. This impressed the Greeks, who disliked most kinds of fish.

[2] Herod. III. 98–99. The "reed" is generally supposed to be the giant bamboo. But no bamboo is large enough to serve this purpose. Hence it has been suggested that the *palmyra tree* is really meant. With its ringed trunk, it was probably mistaken by Skylax and his companions for a kind of bamboo. Megasthenes speaks of "reeds" 180 feet high and three to six cubits in diameter (Strabo, XV. I. 56). Pliny (*N.H.* VII. 2) says a section between two nodes of the Indian reed will make a "dug-out" to carry three men. See McCrindle's learned note to the passage of Strabo, *Ancient India*, pp. 59–60.

[3] Duncker, *Gesch. des. Alt.* II. 268. In the *Rāmāyaṇa* these aborigines figure as "demons" haunting the woods.

[4] *e.g.* the Massagetae, Strabo, XI. 8. 6. Megasthenes also notices this practice among the tribes of the Hindu Kush, Strabo, XV. I. 56.

died in 488 B.C., four years before Herodotus was born[1].

Herodotus is the first writer to mention the famous legend of the Indian ants who watched over the gold which the Indians carried off in order to pay the tribute due to the Great King. It was said that this gold was guarded by gigantic ants, but the Indians, mounted on swift she-camels, plundered the gold at mid-day when the ants were asleep in their holes, and made off, hotly pursued! These "ants" were smaller than dogs but larger than foxes[2], and threw up the gold in excavating their burrows. Some of them were in the possession of the Great King. Later writers talk of having seen their skins[3], or even (*mirabile dictu*) their horns! This curious story arose from the Sanskrit *Paippīlika,* "ant-gold," a term applied to alluvial gold from its resemblance to the earth of ant-hills[4]. The gold was carried off from the

[1] Buddhism spread to the Panjāb very quickly. The people of Gandhāra claimed relationship with Gautama and, as his relatives, a share in his ashes (*Mahāparinibbāna Sutta, S.B.E.* XI. 131).

[2] Pliny says they were of the colour of cats and the size of Egyptian wolves, *N.H.* IX. 31.

[3] Megasthenes *apud* Strabo, XV. I. 44, and Schwanbeck's note *ad loc.* Marten and other skins were early imported from Thibet and central Asia. The famous statue of Anaitis at Baktra was "clothed in beaver-skins."

[4] So Wilson, *Ariana Antiqua,* p. 135, who quotes the *Mahābhārata* (II. 1860) in support. See McCrindle, *Ancient India,* pp. 44 and 51 (notes).

miners of Dardistān, who still keep fierce yellow mastiffs to guard their houses. These mastiffs were the "ants" of the legend. The "horns," which Pliny[1] asserts were hung in the temple of Hercules at Erythrae, were the horns of wild sheep, which, mounted in handles, are still used by the miners and farmers of Ladāk as pickaxes. The gold-fields of Dardistān were quickly exhausted, perhaps by the exorbitant demands of Persia. They are seldom mentioned in later literature[2], though Alexander, had he found them working, would have almost certainly exploited them. To-day they yield only insignificant quantities[3].

On the whole, the account given by Herodotus of the Indian satrapy is careful and accurate. It is no doubt drawn from the lost narrative of Skylax, or from other first-hand evidence[4]. He mentions, among other things, the extremes of heat and cold of the Panjāb, the size of the animals and birds, the crocodiles in the Indus, the horses (which he considers inferior to the Median breed), and the excellent wild-cotton, superior to sheep's

[1] *N.H.* xi. 36.

[2] *e.g.* Pliny's "Fertilissimi sunt auri Derdae" (*N.H.* 19. 67), which may, however, merely be an echo of earlier writers.

[3] Sandrakottus was paid in alluvial gold dust as tribute, probably from the "golden river," the Sona or Hiraṇyabāhu, Strabo, xv. i. 57. It flowed past his capital. He apparently had no gold from the Panjāb.

[4] Probably from the accounts given by Persian officials who had served in India.

wool, of which the Indians made their clothes[1]. Besides the legend of the gold-ants, one or two Indian fables have crept, through Persia, into his narrative. Thus the famous story of Hippokleides[2], who "didn't care" when he danced away his wife, seems to have a close parallel in the *Jātaka* story of the silly young Peacock, who danced so indecently that he shocked the father of the golden Goose, and lost his wealthy bride. The story of the wife of Intaphernes[3], who pleaded for her brother's life, because she could get another son or husband, but not another brother, has been traced to the *Ucchaṅga Jātaka*[4]. The Hyperboreans, who play such a large part in contemporary Greek legend, are the Indian *Uttara-kuru*, transferred rather pointlessly from their home in the holy Himālaya to Europe, where they are quite out of place. Perhaps this legend may be traced to Hekataeus, whose lost work "on the Hyperboreans" is cited by Pliny. It is difficult, however, to see where Hekataeus obtained his information, unless the legend was current in Persia at an early date.

[1] Herodotus was also struck with the *teeming population* of India, which contrasted strongly with the sparsely-inhabited little Greek states. Ἴνδων δὲ πλῆθος πολλῷ πλεῖστον ἐστὶ πάντων τῶν ἡμεῖς ἴδμεν ἀνθρώπων, III. 94. Cf. Strabo, II. 5. 32.

[2] Herod. VI. 110.

[3] Herod. III. 18.

[4] No. 67, Fausböll. See Tawney, *Journal of Philology*, XII. 121.

The praise accorded to Herodotus for the admirable sobriety and truth of his remarks about India, cannot, unfortunately, be extended to Ktesias. Ktesias made very poor use of his opportunities—he was for twenty years court-physician to Artaxerxes Mnemon at Susa, and retired in 398 B.C.[1] He settled in Greece and there wrote his *Indika*, fragments of which survive in the abridgement of Photius and in other writers. It is full of extravagant stories of monstrous people and strange animals, and adds practically nothing to our knowledge of India. Ktesias is responsible for most of the grotesque legends about India which fill the pages of classical and medieval writers to the days of Sir John Mandeville[2]. It may be stated, in excuse, that these fables are repeated, with additions, even by sober writers like Megasthenes, and are not originally due to Greek invention[3]. They were coined in the first instance by the Indians themselves, among whom they apparently originated from exaggerated descriptions of the strange features and repulsive

[1] He was present at the battle of Kunaxa, and treated Artaxerxes for his wound after it. The legends in the *Indika* are treated at length in an appendix to this chapter. The fragments have been edited by Müller and translated by McCrindle.

[2] Othello's "Anthropophagi and men whose heads
Do grow beneath their shoulders."

[3] Nor was Ktesias the first to fall in this respect. Hekataeus mentioned the Skiapodes who used their gigantic feet as umbrellas!

customs of the hated *Dasyus*—aborigines, Dravidian and Mongolian—whom they encountered when the Aryans first invaded India. Thus the Antipodes of Ktesias are the *Paśchādaṅgulajas* of the *Mahābhārata*; the Pygmies are the Kirāta—the Mongolian hillmen of Bhotān or the wild tribes of the Assam frontier perhaps. But this plea will not cover all the sins, of omission and commission, of Ktesias. His Indian animals are as fabulous as his Skiapodes and Anthropophagi. And a reference to the fragments of his companion work, the *Persika*, shews that his other writings were equally unreliable and uncritical. Although he had resided for years in Persia and had the opportunity of consulting the royal archives, he adds little, or nothing, to our knowledge of Persian history. To him, for instance, we owe the fable of the invasion of India by Semiramis and the equally absurd romances attached to the story of the Skythian campaigns of Cyrus the Great.

To the Persians, then, Greece owes her first knowledge of India. Darius had both Greeks and Indians as his subjects. Indian troops formed the light division of the army of Xerxes: they must have marched through the bloody defiles of Thermopylae, and their usefulness caused them to be retained by Mardonius[1] after the retreat of the king, to take part in the Boeotian campaign which ended so disastrously at the Asopus. Ionian officers in Persian employ, and probably Ionian

[1] Herod. VIII. 113.

traders, visited the Panjāb. But with the gradual break-up of the Persian Empire, the practical independence of eastern Irān, and the war with Greece, the traffic between India and the West sank to practically nothing. Probably the satrapy of the Panjāb, like Baktria, owed a merely nominal allegiance, as time went on, to the court at Susa. But the Persian Empire made a profound impression upon the Indian mind. The Kharōshṭhī script, introduced no doubt by the Persians in their official documents, remained in use on the North-West Frontier till the fourth century A.D. The remains of Persian and Babylonian customs at Taxila may point to this place as the capital of the satrapy under the Persian Empire. The Maurya Emperors, as we gather from the account given by Megasthenes of the court of Sandrakottus[1], lived in Persian style. The Indian, like the Persian monarch, lived in seclusion, surrounded by his guards, and only appearing at rare intervals. The Buddhist architecture of Aśoka, with its bell-capitals and winged lions, shews many traces of Persian influence[2]. Aśoka's plan of propagating

[1] Sandrakottus acquired these customs during his long exile in the Panjāb.

[2] And also, of course, that of Assyria through Persia. The fact that the Persian element is so thoroughly assimilated (unlike the crude mixture of East and West in the Gandhāra sculptures) shews that Persian influence had been long felt in India in the days of Aśoka. Persia, no doubt, suggested to Mauryan artists the use of stone instead of wood, brick, and stucco.

the *Dharma* by means of inscriptions upon the face of the rock, may have been borrowed from similar practices in vogue among the Persians —for instance the Behistūn inscription. Even the Royal Road running through the Maurya domains finds its parallel in Persia. How this influence precisely crept in, we are, in our ignorance of the history of the Panjāb at this period, unable to say. Was there a viceregal court at Taxila, where Sandrakottus had seen the stately Persian ceremonial in practice? Or did he merely assume Persian customs, as Alexander and the Syrian Seleukids assumed them, because Persia, even in decay, remained the greatest and most imposing empire known to the world at that time?

APPENDIX

I. KTESIAS. Lassen[1] thinks the current opinion about Ktesias is too harsh, in spite of the fact that he had ample opportunities to question Persian officials who had been to the Panjāb, and confesses to having met certain Indians who had come on an embassy to Persia. Lassen says that we are unable to judge Ktesias fairly from the summary of Photius, as Photius only extracted the marvellous stories. Unfortunately, other writers who had an opportunity of judging the work entire, have recorded their opinion. Thus Aulus Gellius[2], the eminent bibliophile, tells us that he bought a copy of Ktesias on an old bookstall at Brindisium for a few coppers, and was disgusted to find it full of absurd legends. Lucian says that Ktesias wrote about things he had never

[1] *Ind. Alt.* (1874), II. 641. [2] *Noct. Att.* IX. 4.

seen, and had never heard from anyone else. In fact, the testimony of the ancient writers concurs to prove that he set out to write a pleasing narrative after the style of Gulliver's Travels and nothing more. He takes some facts, *e.g.* that the Indians were the last race in the world, from Herodotus[1], and some legends from Skylax. *If* the Hyparkhus is the Ganges, he has the credit for a fresh geographical discovery. He says that the Indus is between 40 and 100 stadia broad; that there are no rains in India, but the land is watered by rivers which overflow like the Nile; that the surface of the sea is too hot for fish to live in it; that there is a spring containing liquid gold. He tells the legend of the gold guarded by griffins.

On Indian plants he is a little more satisfactory. He mentions the cinnamon, giving it its Tamil name *kārppu* (κάρπιον)[2]; also the cocoa-nut, the Indian reed (probably the palmyra, though Lassen says the bamboo), and the fact that there are male and female palms. He mentions cotton, as do most Greek writers on India. He also speaks of the "sweet wine" (*tāḍī*) of the palm[3]. With regard to animals, on the contrary, he indulges in the most ludicrous legends. He speaks fairly sensibly, indeed, of the elephant, the jackal and the parrot. The wild ass, or unicorn[4], whose horn has such wonderful properties, may be the rhinoceros, and the *Skōlēx*, a gigantic worm with two huge teeth, living in the Indus and preying on animals, may be the crocodile. But the descriptions are wildly inaccurate. The *Martichora*, with its triple rows of teeth, the sting in its tail, and other strange attributes,

[1] Lassen denies this. If it is argued that Ktesias could not get more accurate facts, we have only to compare his narrative with that of Herodotus.

[2] Ktesias saw a small quantity of cinnamon oil sent from India as a present. He says it had a most exquisite fragrance. But is he thinking of attar of roses?

[3] He had tasted this and liked it greatly.

[4] καρτάζωον; the Skt. *khaḍga*.

is the man-eating tiger, but the picture is wilfully[1] distorted, almost out of recognition. The dung of the bird *Dikairos*, which produces sleep and even death, can hardly be *opium*, as opium was then unknown in India. The griffin is the gold-guarding ant of the other writers. It has been suggested, though Lassen does not agree, that Ktesias was influenced by the huge mythological animals of the Assyrian sculptures.

Of the Indians, little is worth recording of what has been preserved. The Aryans were fair, they worshipped the Sun and Moon, and lived to a great age—even 200 years! Of the marvellous springs which healed diseases and which revealed the guilty, we hear from other sources. The first were mineral springs; and trial by the ordeal of water is mentioned in the works of the Chinese pilgrims.

The fabulous races, for the legends about which Ktesias is not wholly responsible, are treated in the Appendix to Chapter III.

Photius concludes his summary with the following words: "Ktesias, while romancing in this fashion, asserts that his narrative is literally true, *and declares that he records nothing which he has not seen with his own eyes*, or learnt from the words of many credible witnesses. He adds that he left even greater wonders untold, lest ignorant people might call him a liar!" (*Bibliotheke*, 62. 33). This seems to prove that Ktesias deliberately invented, *pace* Lassen. It is like the tiger which he saw and described.

II. Traces of the Persian Period. Some coins of the Persian Satrapy in the Panjāb survive, *e.g.* the double-daric of Darius Codomannus (337–330 B.C.) figured by Rapson, *Grundriss der Ind.-Ar. Philologie*, Pl. I. 5. At the same time, Athenian *owls* were imported till the closing of the mint in 322 B.C., after which they were imitated locally (*ibid.* Pl. I. 6, 7).

The word *Yavana* occurs in Indian literature first in

[1] *Wilfully*, because Ktesias had *seen* a tiger, sent to the king from India! See Pausanias, IX. 21, and Aristotle, *Hist. Anim.* II. I.

Pānini in the feminine form *Yavanānī*. The commentator Kātyāyana says this is used of *Yavanānī lipi*, the Greek script. Goldstücker, in his learned book on *Pāṇini, his place in Sanskrit Literature* (London, 1861), says Pāṇini was *before Buddha* (568–488 B.C.). But India could hardly have heard of the Greek alphabet before Darius, even though Pāṇini lived in Gandhāra. Goldstücker suggests *cuneiform*, but this is hardly suitable. If, on the other hand, we were to accept the late tradition connecting Pāṇini with the last Nanda king, it would be quite easy to see that Pāṇini was familiar with Greek letters on coins. The expression may possibly be used of *Kharoshṭhī*.

CHAPTER III

THE MAURYA EMPIRE. MEGASTHENES

IN 329 B.C., the long peace of India was rudely disturbed. The army of Alexander entered the Panjāb, and beating down the desperate opposition of the various tribes who tried to bar its way, penetrated to the banks of the Hyphasis. Alexander had now reached the utmost limits of the Persian Empire. Before him lay a vast and unknown country. Some said that the sandy deserts which lay around, stretched to the end of the world, inhabited, perhaps, by the strange monsters described by the pen of Ktesias. Alexander, however, had heard rumours of a vast nation, the Prasii, ruled by a king named Xandrames, who had a mighty army[1], and he was anxious to push on and try conclusions with him.

[1] Plutarch, *Vit. Alex.* 62 The word Prasii, used by Greek writers of the kingdom of Magadha, is probably the Sanskrit *Prāchya,* Eastern. Xandrames may be Nanda Rāja. He is called Angrammes by Curtius (IX. 2). His real name was Mahāpadma. Πράξιοι, Πραίσιοι, Πραΰσιοι, Βρήσιοι, *Pharrasii* are other forms of Πράσιοι, found in Greek and Latin literature (Schwanbeck, p. 82, n.). Cunningham prefers to derive the word from *Parāsa* (*Palāsa*), a name sometimes given to Magadha, derived from the Palāśa tree (*Butea frondosa*).

But the Macedonian troops, desperate at the thought of new terrors and fresh privations, refused to go any further. They had fought battles, crossed deserts and rivers, and climbed mountain ranges at the order of their leader, but this was too much. The breaking-point had been reached at last. And so Alexander had to content himself with the conquest of the old Persian "satrapy of India." He was no mere military adventurer, and from the first his object was to develop the immense commercial resources of the Panjāb. Trading depôts were founded all along the course of the Indus as the Macedonian army moved towards the mouth of the river. Bukephala and Nikaea were built on the banks of the Hydaspes; Alexandria-on-Indus at the important spot where the Akesines joins the main stream; and Patala at the head of the Indus delta[1]. Alexandria-on-Indus soon became an important town. It survived the overthrow of the Macedonian power in the Panjāb for many years, and became famous under the rule of the Baktrian kings as a great Graeco-Buddhist centre. "Alasanda of the Yonas" is mentioned in the *Mahāvaṃsa*, the chronicle-history of the distant island of Ceylon, as the "capital of the Yona country," and 30,000 monks are said to have come from this place to the dedication-festival of the great tope of Ruanvelli

[1] Hence called Patalene. Patala is the modern Bahmanābād. Bukephala is Jihlam. For Alexandria-on-Indus, see Arrian, *Exped. Alex.* VI. 14, 15.

in 137 B.C.[1] We have, curiously enough, in the name of this town, the only mention in Indian literature of the name of the great Macedonian conqueror. Patala remained an important port for western trāde, and was the principal harbour in north-western India until its claims were rivalled by Barygaza. Philip, the satrap of Parthia, was put in charge of the new province, with orders to push on the development of the colonies and the completion of the naval docks and other commercial undertakings with all speed[2]. On reaching the mouth of the river, Alexander determined to build a dock at the end of the eastern arm, as he found there an excellent natural harbour, forming a lake-like basin[3]. Nearchus, the admiral in charge of the Greek fleet, was now sent on to explore the Persian Gulf, while Alexander, undeterred by the legendary stories of the fate of the army of Semiramis, rashly attempted to follow overland across the terrible Mekrān desert.

Arrian gives a diverting account of the perils which beset the fleet at its start, owing to the tidal bore of the Indus, and also to a school of whales, which, sad to say, nearly proved too much for the nerves of the sturdy Macedonian sailors!

[1] See the *Mahāvaṃsa*, trans. Turnour, p. 110, ch. XXIX.

[2] Arrian, *Exped. Alex.* VI. 15. 2.

[3] The course of the river changes so rapidly that we cannot expect to identify any of these places. This is the port to which Nearchus gave the name of *Naustathmos* or Alexander's Haven. It may be the port called by the strange name of *Barbarikon* in the *Periplus*.

Apparently, the government of the Panjāb now fell into the hands of Peithon, while Sind was under Eudamus. Associated with Peithon was Porus, whom Alexander, after his defeat, magnanimously put in this position.

The exploration of the Indus valley was the beginning of a new era in the history of Greek geography, and we cannot help wondering what might have been the result had Alexander lived to carry out his far-reaching schemes. Would the Indus valley have become the centre of Hellenistic culture, as Egypt and Syria became, where the civilization of East and West blended to form new products? The question was destined never to be solved. In June, 323 B.C., the great conqueror died at Babylon of fever.

A wild panic shook the Empire to the centre. No one knew what would happen next, and in the distant colonies of the Panjāb things quickly began to look serious for the Macedonian garrison. A quarrel broke out between Eudamus and his native colleague, which ended in the treacherous assassination of the latter. The death of Porus further exasperated the native population, who broke into open revolt in 317 B.C., when Eudamus and Peithon, taking with them as much loot as they could lay hands on, and the flower of the Macedonian troops, evacuated the Panjāb, and went to join Eumenes in the scramble for power nearer home. No doubt they felt their position to be quite untenable long before they determined upon this move. The revolt was largely organized by Sandrakottus, or Chandragupta, to give him his proper name, the remarkable adventurer who founded the Maurya dynasty[1].

Chandragupta had originally lived in the Panjāb, and a tradition says that as a young man he came into contact with Alexander. He then went to seek his fortune at the court of the Nanda kings of Magadha (there is some reason for supposing that he was of royal blood), and there he met with a fellow-countryman, the crafty Brahmin minister Chāṇakya[2] from Taxila. Becoming implicated in a plot which Chāṇakya had made against his master, he was forced to flee to his former home, and here he found the tribes ripe for revolt against their Greek rulers. Putting himself at the head of the rising, he helped his compatriots, says Justin[3], "to cast off the yoke of servitude from their necks and slay their masters." The people afterwards repented of their choice, he adds, for Chandragupta turned out to be as harsh as those whom he had displaced[4].

[1] There are various stories of the youth of Chandragupta. V. A. Smith (*Early History of India*, p. 110), gives another version. He says that Chandragupta was an illegitimate scion of the Nandas, and was banished to the Panjāb for insolence (Justin, xv. 4, with *Nandrum* for *Alexandrum*).

[2] Also called Kauṭilya and Vishṇugupta.

[3] Post mortem Alexandri, velut cervicibus jugo servitutis excusso, praefectos ejus occiderat. Justin, xv. 4.

[4] Populum, quem ab externa dominatione vindicaverat, ipse servitio premebat. *Ibid.*

By 315 B.C., Macedonian rule in the Panjāb was at an end, though doubtless very considerable bodies of " Yavana " colonists continued to remain settled in the Panjāb, at "Alasanda of the Yonas" and other settlements. They were united by ties of marriage to the country of their adoption and had no desire to return. Having established himself in the Panjāb, Chandragupta marched against Magadha. This time he was successful. The Nanda monarch was defeated, and Chandragupta, with the aid of his old ally Chāṇakya, established himself upon the throne at Pāṭaliputra. He had thus built up for himself a far vaster Empire than India had ever before seen, stretching as it did from the Ganges to the Hindu Kush Mountains. The lessons in imperialism which he had learnt from Alexander had borne good fruit.

How well Chandragupta had used his time was seen in 306 B.C., when Seleukus Nikator tried to repeat the exploits of his former master. He was, however, cruelly disillusioned. On entering the Panjāb, he found himself face to face with a vast and well-organized army, and he was glad to come to terms with his opponent. Chandragupta, on the other hand, was alive to the advantages of an agreement with the Syrian monarch, and an alliance was arranged. Chandragupta was to receive certain provinces in Arachosia and Gedrosia over which Syria had long ceased to exercise a *de facto* sovereignty, while Seleukus was given six hundred elephants to aid him in his war against Antigonus.

He hoped for great results from this new and formidable arm. The alliance between the monarchs was cemented by a marriage between the Indian king and a Syrian princess. Such a daring innovation is in itself a convincing proof of the greatness of Chandragupta's mind. It was probably owing to this occurrence that the Syrian and Maurya monarchs continued for several generations to maintain a close and friendly intercourse. An amusing correspondence, of which a fragment or two is recorded, was maintained between Bindusāra and Seleukus. Bindusāra asks for a sample of Greek wine, some raisins and a "Sophist." Seleukus writes back, saying that he sends the wine with much pleasure, but regrets that "it isn't good form among the Greeks to trade in philosophers[1]!" When Aśoka was converted to Buddhism, his first thought was to despatch missionaries to his friends, the Greek monarchs of Egypt, Syria and Macedonia, that they might share in the glad tidings of his new creed. Ambassadors from the West frequently visited the Maurya court. Megasthenes came from Seleukus to Chandragupta; Dēimachus from the same monarch to Bindusāra, Chandragupta's son and successor, and Dionysius from Ptolemy Philadelphus[2]. The most important of these, of course, was Megasthenes, to whom we owe the only complete account we possess of the court and government of the great

[1] Müller, *Frag. Hist. Graec.* IV. 421.

[2] Pliny, *N.H.* VI. 17. 3. Strabo, II. I. 10.

Indian monarch. His work, though no longer extant, is known to us from numerous citations by Strabo, Pliny, Arrian, Diodorus, Photius and others[1].

Megasthenes was originally stationed at the court of Syburtius, satrap of Arachosia[2]. He was ordered to proceed to India about 302 B.C. Whether he also visited the court of another Indian prince, to whom the generic name of "Porus" is given[3], and whether he paid one or many visits to the Maurya monarch[4], is not quite certain. "He dwelt for some time," says Solinus, "with Indian kings, and wrote a History of India, that he might hand down to posterity a faithful account of what he saw there." The credibility of his narrative was generally accepted in ancient times, —Arrian calls him a "trustworthy person[5]"— though the sceptical Strabo, disgusted by the impossibility of distinguishing truth from falsehood in the many conflicting accounts of India, roundly calls

[1] Collected by Schwanbeck (Bonn, 1846). For the life of Megasthenes, see the introduction to this work, and the Preface to Müller's edition.

[2] See Arrian, *Exped. Alex.* v. 6. 2.

[3] Schwanbeck emends *Πώρῳ ἔτι τούτου μείζονι* to *Πώρου ἔτι τούτῳ μείζονι*, "Greater even than Porus."

[4] Πολλάκις δὲ λέγει Μεγασθένης ἀφικέσθαι παρὰ Σανδράκοττον. (Arrian, *Exped. Alex.* v. 6. 2). This may mean that Megasthenes often *went* to Pāṭaliputra, or often *visited* Chandragupta when at Pāṭaliputra.

[5] δόκιμος ἀνήρ. He classes him with Eratosthenes. Strabo, who has the highest opinion of Eratosthenes, differs entirely from this view.

him a liar, almost as untrustworthy as Dēimachus[1]. Pliny shares his opinion[2]. As a matter of fact, Megasthenes has now been completely vindicated. His description of India agrees wonderfully with what we have learnt from independent Indian sources, and the only justification of Strabo's censures is to be found in his account of the fabulous races of India. And here Megasthenes, like his predecessors, is not wholly to blame. He repeats legends which were current in India, and he took them in perfect good faith from his informants, as may be seen from the fact that their names are all literal translations of Sanskrit words[3]. Megasthenes is, of course, only reliable as far as he saw the country with his own eyes. Thus he is unaware of the existence of the great Ganges delta, as he never descended that river below Pāṭaliputra[4]. He states that, unlike the Indus, the Ganges has only a *single* mouth[5]!

[1] "As a rule, previous writers about India have been a pack of liars. Dēimachus comes first and Megasthenes next," *Geog.* II. I. 9. But the veracity of Megasthenes is established by comparison with the *Kauṭilīya Artha Śāstra* and other Indian works (*vide* App. III).

[2] Pliny, *N.H.* VI. 12. 3, "It is not worth while to study the accounts of Megasthenes and Dionysius with care. They are too conflicting and too incredible."

[3] The stories of the fabulous tribes of India are as old as Hekataeus. See what is said upon the subject in Chapter II. A list of the fabulous tribes is given in Appendix II to this chapter.

[4] Arrian, *Indika*, V.

[5] Megasthenes *apud* Strabo, *Geog.* XV. I. 13.

The first thing which struck Megasthenes on entering India, was the Royal Road from the frontier to Pāṭaliputra, down which the envoy must have travelled to the capital[1]. It was constructed in eight stages, and ran from the frontier town of Peukelaotis[2] to Taxila: from Taxila, across the Indus to the Jihlam; then to the Beās, near the spot where Alexander erected his altars. From here it went to the Sutlej: from the Sutlej to the Jamnā: and from the Jamnā, probably *viâ* Hastināpura, to the Ganges. From the Ganges the road ran to a town called Rhodopha[3], and from Rhodopha to Kalinipaxa (probably Kanyākubja or Kanauj)[4]. From Kanauj it went to the mighty town of Prayāga at the junction of the Ganges and the Jamnā, and from Prayāga to Pāṭaliputra. From the capital it continued its course to the mouth of the Ganges, probably at Tāmluk, though Megasthenes never traversed the last stage of the road. At every mile along the road was a stone to indicate the by-roads and distances. The road was in the charge of the officers of the Board of Works who were responsible for its upkeep. The milestones were of great assistance to geographers in the computation of the distances between places

[1] See Pliny, *N.H.* VI. 21, and Appendix at the end of this chapter.

[2] The capital of Gandhāra (Skt. *Pushkalāvatī*).

[3] Said to be Dabhai near Anupshahr.

[4] So Lassen. St Martin says *Kālīnī-paksha*, a town supposed to be on the "side" of the Kālīnadī.

in India. There seems to be little doubt that this road was one of the many schemes emanating from the master-mind of the great Maurya Emperor, though he may have utilized to some extent existing routes, which he linked up for the purpose[1]. The idea may have been suggested by the Royal Road of Persia, and may be reckoned as one of the many signs of Persian influence in the Maurya Empire. Its value, from a commercial as well as a strategic point of view, must have been enormous. By means of it, troops could be moved from Pāṭaliputra to the furthest confines of the Empire; it joined up all the great cities—Taxila, Kanauj, Hastināpura, Prayāga—with the capital; and by it trade was immensely facilitated. Goods from the Golden Chersonese and beyond, silk from the Seres, Gangetic muslins, spices from Arabia, specie from the West, all poured into the bazaars of Pāṭaliputra, and caravans could pass uninterrupted from the Ganges to the Khaibar. The prosperity of the foreign trade is attested by the elaborate regulations made by Chandragupta for the entertainment of foreign merchants[2].

Along this great highway Megasthenes travelled into lands never before beheld by Greek eyes. At last he came in sight of the broad stream of the

[1] That some such road as far as the Beās existed in the days of Alexander is of course implied in the statement that he obtained the measurements from the records of Alexander's survey officers. A road from Ayodhya to Rājagṛiha, *viâ* Hastināpura, is mentioned in the *Rāmāyaṇa*.

[2] Megasthenes *apud* Strabo, XV. I. 51.

sacred Ganges, and his exaggerated accounts of its size—he says it was eight or ten miles wide in places[1]—testify to his wonder at beholding it. The Greeks, having no rivers of any note in their own lands, were filled with admiration at the sight of such streams as the Nile, the Euphrates, the Ganges or the Indus. He was struck with the fertility of the Doāb through which the road passes, with its two crops and two monsoons every year[2]. Like Herodotus, he remarks on the hugeness of the animals—the elephants, pythons, tigers, and hunting-hounds[3]—and the curious plants and trees—the "reed" (really, as we have seen before, the palmyra) out of which boats could be made; the banyan with its spreading branches; the "vegetable wool" or cotton[4], the "honey bearing reed," or sugar-cane, and the ubiquitous rice-plant.

At length Megasthenes came in sight of the Royal City. It stood at the junction of the Ganges and the Son[5], and presented an imposing appearance[6]. It was in the shape of a parallelogram, and

[1] Megasthenes *apud* Pliny, VI. 18. 65. Arrian (*Indika*, IV) states that according to Megasthenes, the Ganges in places spreads out into lakes which are so wide that it is impossible to see from shore to shore! It is difficult to believe that Megasthenes made such a statement. See Schwanbeck, *Frag.* XX. B and XXV.

[2] Strabo, XV. I. 20 (*Frag.* XI, Schwan.).

[3] Schwanbeck, *Frag.* XII–XVII, sums up all the passages on Indian animals.

[4] If this is what Arrian means by λίνον τὸ ἀπὸ δένδρεων. Flax and cotton are continually confused.

[5] The river has since altered its course.

[6] Pāṭaliputra is described in *Fragments* XXV and XXVI, Schwan. (Arrian, *Indika*, X, and Strabo, XV. I. 35.)

was surrounded by vast walls of brick, with a wooden palisade in front, pierced with loopholes for archery. The wall had sixty-four gates and five hundred and seventy towers; it was eighty stadia long on its longer sides, and fifteen stadia long on the shorter. On the two sides not protected by the rivers, ran a huge moat, filled with the waters of the Son, into which it flowed. This moat, six hundred feet broad and thirty cubits deep, protected the town and also carried off the drainage. The city was one of the strongest in the world, but like most of the towns of India at that time, it was built chiefly of wood and unburnt brick. It was the custom, says Megasthenes, to use wood where floods were common, and brick and mud when the buildings were on elevated spots. This is the reason why so little has survived of the early architecture of India. Two generations later, the use of stone became common, and Aśoka crowned the capital with a gigantic stone palace, exquisitely carved. Centuries afterwards, a Chinese pilgrim, wandering among the ruins of the then deserted city, gazed with awe upon the huge stone blocks scattered here and there, and declared that they could be the work of "no mortal hands." Excavations are now proceeding upon the site of Pāṭaliputra, and the accuracy of the account of Megasthenes has received fresh confirmation. The wall and palisade were unearthed some years ago.

Of the court of Chandragupta, with its

ceremonies, and of his system of administration, we have a highly interesting and detailed description in Megasthenes. Chandragupta was by no means popular. His rule, as we have seen before, was considered tyrannous and oppressive. The easy-going and indolent Indians, no doubt, disliked a highly-organized system of government to which they were unused; and the foreign air of the court, with its Greek inmates, and its Persian ceremonial, did not help to ingratiate the monarch with his subjects. Megasthenes, whose account is confirmed by Indian writers[1], says that he was obliged to dwell in strict seclusion. He was surrounded by a body-guard of women, who cooked his food, served his wine, and when of an evening he had become weary, carried him to his apartments and lulled him to sleep with Indian music[2]. Even at night he was constantly compelled to change his bedroom, to avoid the attacks of possible conspirators, who, according to native tradition, even dug tunnels under the palace walls[3]. In the day he sat in the Hall of Justice, hearing complaints, while his attendant[4] massaged him with wooden rollers, rubbed scented ointments on his feet, and combed and dressed his long hair.

[1] *Mudrā Rākshasa*, Act II. This play is a most interesting historic drama, and throws many sidelights on Chandragupta's career.

[2] Strabo, XV. I. 55. Q. Curtius, VIII. 9 (*Frag.* XXVII, Schwanbeck).

[3] *Mudrā Rākshasa* (*loc. cit.*).

[4] *Saṃvāhaka.*

It was at this time that the foreign ambassadors were received, and Megasthenes must have attended many a time the strange levée which he here so graphically describes. On the rare occasions when the monarch left the seclusion of the Royal Palace, whether to offer sacrifice or to go hunting, his Amazonian guard accompanied him, forming a hedge round the royal chariot. One or two women, armed to the teeth, rode in the chariot, while others were mounted on horses or elephants. The road when the royal *cortège* was to pass was marked off with ropes, and a ring of spearmen surrounded the whole retinue. No one was allowed to approach, and it was certain death for any, man or woman, to pass the barriers[1]. Megasthenes says that these women were bought from their parents and brought up in the palace; but it is more probable that they were partly foreign, and mostly Westerners. Greek girls, we know, were frequently imported at Barygaza[2], and a "Guard of Yavana women" is a stock feature of the Rāja's court in the Indian dramas[3]. In Southern India, we hear of a body-guard of "dumb Mlecchas" being used in a similar fashion[4]. Their utility was obvious;

[1] τῷ δὲ παρέλθοντι ἐντὸς μεχρὶ γυναικῶν θάνατος. *Frag.* XXVII, Schwan.

[2] *Periplus*, § 49.

[3] Dushyanta Rāja, *e.g.* has such a guard in the *Śakuntalā* of Kālidāsa. So Chandragupta himself, *Mudrā Rākshasa*, Act III.

[4] Vincent Smith, *Early Hist. of India*, p. 400. Pillay, *The Tamils a eighteen Hundred years ago*, Ch. III.

they were foreign mercenaries, and as such, likely to be loyal to their employer and unwilling to plot against him. They had no motive for taking sides in any disputes, and being unable to understand much of the language of the country, had no sympathies with any political party. They have been compared, not inaptly, with the "Switzers," the Swiss Guards of the French monarchs, and the Swiss mercenaries of other kings.

Chandragupta lived in considerable state. In the processions held on festal occasions, elephants decked in gold and silver, four-horsed chariots, and yokes of oxen took part. "Then comes a great host of attendants in holiday dress, with golden vessels such as huge basins and goblets, six feet broad, tables, chairs of state, drinking vessels and lavers, all of Indian copper, and many of them set with jewels such as emeralds, beryls and Indian garnets; others bear robes embroidered in gold thread, and lead wild beasts, such as buffaloes, leopards and tame lions, and rare birds in cages[1]." "In the Indian royal palace," says another writer, "where the greatest of all the kings of the country resides, besides much else which is calculated to excite admiration, there are wonders with which neither Memnonian Susa in all its glory, nor the magnificence of Ekbatana can

[1] Strabo, XV. I. 69. This was no doubt a copy of the Persian ceremonial which was generally adopted at Oriental courts. See *e.g.* the account of the processions of Antiochus Epiphanes and Ptolemy Philadelphus in Athenaeus, IV. 4. 5.

hope to vie ; indeed, only the well-known vanity of the Persians could imagine such a comparison[1]."

Of the army of Chandragupta, the famous force which defeated Seleukus Nikator, Megasthenes gives us a very full account[2]. Its numbers are possibly exaggerated, as is the size of nearly everything in India by the Greeks. It consisted of cavalry, infantry, chariots and elephants[3], and its total number was said to be 400,000. Possibly this includes the grooms, buglers, gong-beaters, ox-drivers, mechanics and foragers—the vast array of suttlers which follows an oriental army. It was managed by a very efficient War Office, with a department in charge of each arm of the service. There were stables for the horses, chariots and elephants, and magazines where all arms had to be stored when not in use. The chariots on the march were drawn by oxen, so as to keep the horses fresh : in battle, two men-at-arms stood by the driver, and each elephant carried four sharpshooters. The horses were driven with a spiked muzzle, a halter instead of a bridle, and the infantry were armed with long shields of undressed oxhide, two-handed swords, and bows of great length and power, which they discharged by resting them on the ground against the left foot.

[1] Aelian, περὶ ζώων ἰδιότητος, Bk XIII. 18. I.

[2] See Arrian, *Indika*, XVI, and *Fragments* XXXIII and XXXIV Schwanbeck (Strabo, XV. I. 50, and Aelian, XIII. 10).

[3] The four *kāya, aśvakāya, pattikāya, rathakāya* and *hastikāya*.

The arrow, three yards long, pierced shield and armour like paper. They carried two-handed swords, but did not care for closing with the enemy. The cavalry, who had no saddles, had two long lances (σαύνια) as their chief equipment. The army, which was a standing one, was liberally paid, and the soldiers spent much of their time drinking and idling.

We now turn to the very interesting account given by Megasthenes of the organization of the Government, where again we see the work of the master-mind of the great Maurya[1]. Megasthenes gave a minute account of this elaborate system, which has been copied by many subsequent authorities. Unfortunately, he mixes up the traditional four castes of Hindu society[2] with the official bodies created by Chandragupta, and he becomes confused over the sub-castes, with their perplexing distribution of functions in the state. The mistake was not an unnatural one for a foreigner to make. He is also led astray by the fact that the Egyptians, according to Herodotus, had seven castes. Egypt and India were frequently confused by the Greeks, and Megasthenes comes to the conclusion that there are seven "castes" (γένη) in India also[3]. He arrives at this number as follows. He divides the Brahmins into two castes—philosophers and

[1] Schwanbeck, *Frag.* I, XXXIII, and XXXIV. (Diodorus, II. 40; Strabo, XV. I. 39; Arrian, *Indika*, XI.)

[2] Brāhmaṇa, Kshattriya, Vaiśya, Śūdra.

[3] Γένος is a literal translation of *jāti*.

statesmen. The Kshattriyas or Military form a caste by themselves. The Vaiśyas and Śūdras are divided into three castes by Megasthenes—farmers, herdsmen, and artisans, and he adds a seventh caste of "Inspectors and Overseers"—the confidential officers in the service of Chandragupta[1]. These officials were probably recruited chiefly from the Brahmin caste.

First in order, in the catalogue of Megasthenes, came the *Philosophers* (Φιλόσοφοι, Σοφισταί) employed in literary and scientific pursuits and religious rites. These were, of course, the Brahmins, ubiquitous as ever. Of the religion and philosophy of the Brahmins, Megasthenes speaks in another place, and the subject will be treated separately. Once a year a great conclave of Brahmins was held by the king, when rewards were dispensed to those who had produced literary works or made scientific discoveries of merit[2].

Then came the *Husbandmen* (Γεωργοί). Megasthenes found the Indian rayat to be, as he is now, of a peaceful, gentle nature. Exempted from military service, he took no part in war and politics, and lived quietly on his farm, rarely going to the city. Often, says Megasthenes, you

[1] The *Pativedakā* of Aśoka.

[2] Megasthenes may be thinking of the great fairs held at places like Prayāga once a year. Hiuen Tsiang describes one which he attended with king Śilāditya. The monarch distributed gifts to many thousands of Brahmins, monks, and mendicants.

might see him calmly ploughing, while contending armies a little distance off were fighting for their lives. India changes little, and when the English troops were besieging Delhi in 1857, the ploughman went on with his work between the Ridge and the doomed city, just as Megasthenes describes him as doing. So complete is the division of labour brought about by the caste-system. It is interesting to note that all land belonged to the Crown. There was no private ownership[1]. As in all ancient communities, the taxation was severe. The rayat paid the Crown three-fourths, or according to others, one-fourth of the produce, in addition to ground-rent (χώρας μισθοί).

The third class consisted of *Herdsmen*[2], and included shepherds, hunters, and various people of that kind. They were mostly members of the aboriginal tribes, and as such, belonged to the Śūdras, the lowest stratum of Hindu society. They rendered, however, important services to the State. They cleared the fields of the tigers, boars, deer, and birds, which molested the villagers' flocks, herds, and crops. They killed the snakes, scorpions, and dangerous insects which infested the country in the rainy season. Most important of all, they caught and tamed the elephants which played such an important part in the army of

[1] In many places a village held land in common and the crops were divided. This is a survival of the primitive Indo-Aryan village-community. Strabo, XV. I. 66.

[2] βουκόλοι καὶ ποιμένες καὶ καθόλου πάντες οἱ νομέες. Diod. Sic.

Chandragupta. In return for their services, they received an allowance of corn from the Royal Exchequer. Private people were forbidden to keep elephants, which were reserved for royal use. This served as a sumptuary law, checking the ambitions of the nobility; it also secured the maximum number of these valuable beasts for the imperial forces.

The fourth class consisted of the *Artizans* (τεχνῖται). These, according to the code of Manu, were Vaiśyas, like the Agriculturalists. This class included the great Trade-Guilds, many of which received land and other privileges in return for service rendered to the State. Thus the Armourers and Shipwrights had a monopoly of work in their own branches, receiving wages and rations in payment; and taxes were wholly or partly remitted to State employés. In time of peace, the Admiralty hired out their men of war to merchants to be employed on the flourishing traffic in goods and passengers which went on along the Ganges and Jamnā, and doubtless along the waters of the Indus as well.

The fifth caste was the *Military Caste*[1], the Kshattriyas of the Hindu codes. The immense standing army of Chandragupta gave special prominence to members of this caste, who were liberally treated in the matter of pay and allowances. Accoutrements were found by the War Office, which had a special contract with the

[1] Πολεμισταί.

armourers' guild. Weapons were kept in the arsenals, under the supervision of the Ordnance Department.

Sixthly came the *Overseers*[1] or *Inspectors*, a branch of the Civil Service specially maintained by Chandragupta. These officers travelled round inspecting the work of the government officials, and furnishing confidential reports direct to the Throne on their conduct. They spied on the army too, and it is said that they freely used the courtezans of the city to obtain information[2]. Besides keeping the Viceroys and rulers of the distant provinces of the great Empire up to the mark, they no doubt checked the frequent plots hatched against the Emperor's life. When they were on circuit, they gave even the meanest subject a chance to appeal against official tyranny. The post is said to have been a well-paid one, and much in request among adventurous youths. It seems probable that Aśoka used these officials to enforce the Law of the *Dharma* on his subjects.

The seventh and last class was that of the *Royal Councillors*, the ministers who formed the Privy Council of the Emperor. Like the philosophers of the first class, they must have been all, or nearly all, Brahmins, but Megasthenes distinguishes between those Brahmins who devoted themselves to priestly and literary occupations, and those who, like the great Chāṇakya, made politics their

[1] Ἔφοροι, Ἐπίσκοποι.

[2] Strabo, XV. I. 48.

occupation, and became, as priests in many countries have done, the power behind the throne. Nearchus observed this. " Some of the Brahmins," he says, "enter political life and attend the king as councillors, while others devote themselves to philosophy[1]." This class had the monopoly of the great offices of State—posts as " Judge, governor, deputy-governor, ruler over a province, quaestor, superintendent of agriculture, admiral or general," says Arrian.

Apart from the seven classes into which the State was divided, was the Civil Service proper. In rural districts, the government was in the hands of a body of officials, who combined the duties of the Collector, Forest Officer, and Engineer of modern India. These officers had the most varied duties. They superintended irrigation, the construction of irrigation works, and the survey and assessment of irrigated lands. They saw to the repair of public roads, and to the erection of milestones and signposts at every ten stadia. They built and repaired the bridges. They collected the taxes imposed upon the rayats: they supervised the hunters, and saw that they did not defraud the State of horses or elephants. They kept an eye on the wood-cutters and took care that the country was not deforested. They supervised the mines. They appear to have been invested with the judicial powers necessary for the enforcement of their decrees.

[1] Strabo, XV. I. 66.

The system in vogue in the rural districts was of a simple kind, reminding us in a primitive manner of the modern Civil Service, with its multifarious duties. The system of urban government was more complicated. We have Megasthenes' account of the administration of Pāṭaliputra: no doubt Taxila, Ujjain, Prayāga, and the other provincial capitals and great cities, were governed in a similar fashion. There were six *panchāyats*, or boards of five officers, and each board had its own department allotted to it. Besides this, the whole municipal council of thirty members met from time to time to discuss common measures, such as the repair of roads, upkeep of markets, temples and so forth, and to fix the taxes and the current market prices.

The first, fourth, fifth and sixth boards devoted their attention to commercial regulations. The first supervised industries, crafts, trade-guilds, and so on. The fourth board superintended the markets, saw that the weights and measures were duly tested and stamped, and that the proper fixed prices were charged. A curious regulation, due to the specialization resulting from the caste system, imposed a double tax on merchants selling two kinds of goods. The fifth body supervised manufactures, and prevented the frauds arising from adulteration. The sixth was employed in levying the tax of one-tenth upon all articles sold. It is a tribute at once to the Hindu reputation for probity and to the severity of Chandragupta's system, that death was the penalty for a false declaration of sales[1].

To the second and third boards were assigned peculiar duties. The second board was charged with the task of seeing to the comfort of all travellers, merchants, ambassadors, and other foreigners visiting India[2]. They had to attend them when sick, bury them if they died, and send their effects to their relatives in their native country. The existence of this board points to the supposition that a large number of merchants, chiefly, no doubt, Greeks from Syria and Alexandria, visited India in this reign, attracted by Chandragupta's far-sighted foreign policy. The last board of officials managed the census reports, and registered births and deaths. By this means taxation was facilitated, and the practice of infanticide, common among certain classes of Hindus, was checked. The penalties imposed for various offences were terribly severe. We can only suppose that owing to the high level of morality prevailing in India, they were seldom inflicted. No doubt, however, Chandragupta's severity accounts very largely for his unpopularity. Maiming—a Persian form of punishment—was imposed for perjury. The death-penalty was, as we have seen, exacted for the comparatively trifling offence of defrauding the

1 Manu, who does not mention the penalty, puts the tax at $\frac{1}{20}$. Evidently the system was later relaxed. Chandragupta's laws were in all respects exceptionally severe for India.

2 Compare the duties of the Greek πρόξενος, by whom this office was doubtless suggested.

revenue, and also for disabling a craftsman. Even Aśoka retained the death-penalty, but he gave the criminal three days' respite for religious exercises. Apparently, in Chandragupta's time, sentence was carried into execution as soon as passed. In the days of Fa-Hian, capital punishment had been removed from the statute-book.

One feature of Hindu society struck Megasthenes with admiration. Slavery, a universal custom in the Graeco-Roman world, was unknown. Had Megasthenes, however, seen the social conditions of the Chaṇḍāla or Pariah in the days of Hiuen Tsiang, he might have modified his opinions. Under the caste-system, the wretched Pariah, compelled to dwell outside the city-walls, and to strike a gong when he came within range of respectable men, fared far worse than the Greek or Roman slave. But in the days when Buddhism was a growing force in the land, caste regulations were doubtless less rigidly enforced.

Of the moral tone of Hindu society as he saw it, Megasthenes speaks in the highest terms. Hindus lived frugal, happy lives. Wine was never drunk except at the sacrifices, when the *Soma* juice was consumed by the priests. The chief article of food was rice-pottage. Polygamy was indeed common among the upper classes, but women enjoyed great liberty. They studied philosophy, and could take monastic vows[1]. The seclusion of

[1] Strabo, XV. I. 66. Gautama, we are told, made this concession, but unwillingly.

the female sex was only introduced in Mohammedan times. *Satī*, the terrible custom so common in later India, was only practised among two tribes, and is mentioned as a curiosity, whence we may conclude that it was very unusual. It was confined to the Kathaei and to Taxila. The Kathaei were no doubt a Rājput tribe, who left the Amritsar district and occupied the modern Kathiāwār at a later period. *Satī* has always been commonest among that stern and warlike nation. Suicide, chiefly by burning, was always occasionally practised among Buddhist ascetics, though strictly forbidden by Gautama himself[1].

The Indians enjoyed a great and well-founded reputation for probity. Of their honesty, Megasthenes, like Hiuen Tsiang many centuries later, speaks in an extraordinarily enthusiastic fashion. When he visited the camp of Chandragupta, he found that, in the whole of the vast army encamped there, the thefts reported amounted to the value of less than 200 *drachmae* per day[2]. They left their houses unguarded, made no written contracts, and no written laws. They seldom went to law. Legal cases were decided according to immemorial custom by the local *panchāyat*. Strabo notes that the

[1] The standard example was Kalanos, the notorious philosopher who returned with Alexander to Babylon. See *Frag.* XLIV, XLV, LV, etc. in Schwanbeck.

[2] Γενόμενος δ' οὖν ἐν τῷ Σανδρακόττου στρατοπέδῳ φησὶν ὁ Μεγασθένης τετταράκοντα μυριάδων πλήθους ἱδρυομένου μηδεμίαν ἡμέραν ἰδεῖν ἀνηνεγμένα κλέμματα πλείονα ἢ διακοσίων δραχμῶν ἔξω. Strabo, XV. I. 53. The drachma is worth a franc.

Hindus were acquainted with reading and writing, and used paper woven from flax. This we should, of course, infer from the existence of Aśoka's Edicts. Strabo also mentions the contrary opinion, which no doubt arose from the comparative rarity of written books. Laws, religious precepts, even secular poetry were committed to memory and handed down orally. Fa-Hian had to travel all over India before he could obtain texts of the Buddhist Canon.

The people of Pāṭaliputra dressed well in flowered muslins embroidered with jewels, and an umbrella was carried by an attendant behind the head of a noble when he went into the road. Kleitarchus, however, found that in other, poorer parts of India, they wore fillets (turbans, no doubt), on their long hair, and robes of plain white muslin or linen[1].

Of the ancient history of India, Megasthenes apparently learnt nothing worth recording, save legends of a monarch whom he identified with Bacchus or Herakles. This is not surprising, as the science of history was always entirely neglected by the Hindus. Of the religion of the country he gives an interesting and intelligent account. The principal religious sects were the Brahmins, and the Sarmanes, who were the Buddhists and Jains. Besides these, there were, then as now, various *fakirs*, *Yogis*, and other mendicants of a low type, who had considerable liberty in the houses and markets, helping themselves in the

[1] Strabo, XV. I. 71.

bazaars to what they liked. Of Brahmin philosophy, we do not find so full an account in Megasthenes as in later writers[1]. The charming fragment quoted from the pseudo-Origen by Schwanbeck[2], appears to owe little to Megasthenes, being Neo-platonic in tone. Megasthenes notes, however, the similarity between the speculations of the Brahmins and the teachings of Pythagoras and Plato; he speaks also of their physical speculations, and their belief that the world is spherical, liable to destruction, and permeated by the presence of the Deity[3]. They also, he says, believed in the existence of a fifth element—the Ākāśa or ether. These philosophers, he tells us, were devotees of Herakles, and there was a tribe called the Sibae, who were the descendants of the companions of Herakles. Herakles must be Śiva and the Sibae a Śaivite sect. The Greeks loved to identify the gods of other nations with their own deities. Indra is "Zeus Ombrios"; the immoral *Śakti* rites of certain tribes (*e.g.* the Oxydrakae) are the Bacchic orgies, and so forth. It has even been thought that the name of Mount Meru, suggesting the Μηρός of the Bacchus legend, went a long way

[1] Schwanbeck, *Frag.* XLI–XLIII. [2] *Ibid.* LIV.

[3] A good example of the out-of-the-way information gleaned by Megasthenes is given by Strabo, XV. I. 59. "The Brahmins from the time of conception in the womb are under the care of learned men who go to the mother with incantations for the welfare of herself and her offspring." Here is a clear reference to the *Puṃ-Savana* and *Garbha-Rakshaṇa* of the *Gṛihya Sūtras*. (Barnett, *Indian Antiq.* Ch. IV.)

towards confirming, in Greek minds, the persistent belief that Bacchus came from India.

Buddhism was not so popular in the days of Megasthenes as it afterwards became under the vigorous advocacy of Aśoka. Megasthenes says nothing of the distinctive teachings of the *Sarmanes*. Their most distinguished members were the Hylobioi (*Vānaprastha*), who retired to the forest and lived on the bark of trees. Megasthenes apparently fails to distinguish Brahminism from Buddhism, as this is a Hindu and not a Buddhistic practice. Among the philosophers, Megasthenes reckons the physicians, who appear to have attained to a high degree of proficiency. No doubt the difficulties of ascertaining much about Hindu philosophy were very great for a foreigner. As the sage Mandanis remarks to Onesikritus, "It is impossible to explain philosophical doctrines through the medium of interpreters who know nothing of the subject. It is like asking water to flow pure through mud[1]."

Such then, in brief, is the interesting account of the great Maurya Empire as it appeared to the first Greek who penetrated to the heart of India. Its value to us is shown by the fact that without it our knowledge of this important period would be practically a blank. By comparing what Megasthenes has said with the Edicts of Aśoka and the *Artha Śāstra* of Chāṇakya, we are able to form a clear picture of the general character

[1] Strabo, xv. I. 64, *fin*.

of Maurya institutions. We see a highly organized government, and a nation distinguished for its probity and intelligence. The work of Megasthenes refutes the popular idea that because India has no history, she has been incapable of developing political institutions.

We have seen that the Maurya Emperors were in close touch with their Greek neighbours and kinsmen. Chandragupta has a Greek wife, Greek ambassadors in his court, and corresponds with the Syrian monarch. Aśoka sends missionaries to his Greek neighbours. And yet, when we examine the matter closely, we find little trace of Greek influence in India at the time of the Mauryas. On the other hand, they were deeply influenced by the now vanished Persian Empire. For centuries the Persians had ruled in the Panjāb, and the Indians had been impressed by the stately edifice of Persian rule. Perhaps Chandragupta had, during his boyhood in Taxila, come under Persian influence. The customs of his court were purely Persian. Like the Great King, he lived in seclusion, only appearing for religious festivals and on solemn occasions. He kept, like him, the "hair-washing festival," *Tykta*, described by Herodotus[1]. Many other institutions of Chandragupta had their Persian parallels, for instance, the Royal Road, and probably the provincial organization. Then again, we see Persian influence in the architectural undertakings of Aśoka. The Edicts

[1] Herod. IX. 110 and Strabo, XV. I. 69.

engraved on the rock may be compared to the Behistūn inscriptions of Darius, and the lion capitals of the Aśoka pillars are clearly Persian in style, though that style has undergone considerable modification.

APPENDIX I

THE ROYAL ROAD

Pliny (VI. 21) says that the stages and distances on the Royal Road are as follows:

1. From Peukelaotis to the Hyphasis, as measured by Baeto and Diognetus, Alexander's survey officers.

Peukelaotis to Taxila, 60 miles.
,, the Hydaspes, 120 miles.
,, the Hyphasis, 390 miles.

2. From the Hyphasis to the mouth of the Ganges, as measured for Seleukus Nikator (probably by Megasthenes and other Greek visitors[1]).

From the Hyphasis to the Hēsidrus	168 miles.
From the Hēsidrus to the Jamnā	168 miles (some add 5).
From the Jamnā to the Ganges	112 miles.
From the Ganges to Rhodopha	119 miles (others give 325[2]).

Then follow the words "*Ad Kalinapaxam oppidum* CLXVII.D *Alii* CCLXV. *mill.*" This is usually translated, "To the town of Kallinapaxa 167½ miles; others 265 miles," which seems a curious discrepancy. St Martin (*Étude sur la Géog. Grecque,*

[1] "Reliqua Seleuko Nikatori peragrata sunt." This is of course a *dativus commodi, not* a dative of the agent. Seleukus never went beyond the Panjāb.

[2] By 325 miles he must mean for the *whole* distance from the Hēsidrus to Rhodopha, *not* from the Ganges. He refers to a shorter route, the longer route being 168 + 112 + 119 = 399 miles. There were several short cuts, marked by signposts, on the road.

Aśoka Pillar (Indo-Persian)

(By permission of the Director General of Archaeology)

p. 271), transfers the D to the latter clause, reading DLXV for CCLXV. He then translates as follows. " From Rhodopha to Kallinapaxa 167 miles. *Total from the Hēsidrus to Kallinapaxa* 565 miles." This is ingenious if bold, for the total figures from the Hēsidrus to Kallinapaxa (168 + 112 + 119 + 167) *do* add up to 566 miles—practically the exact figure.

He next goes on to say that to Prayāga is 625 miles (many add 13). He must mean from the Jamnā to Prayāga, of course, and not from Kallinapaxa.

His two last statements are absolutely wide of the mark. He says it is 425 miles to Palibothra and 638 miles to the mouth of the Ganges. The distances are in reality 248 and 445 miles respectively. The latter part of the road had not been travelled by Megasthenes, who puts it at 500–600 miles. In the absence of definite information, the Greeks always exaggerated the size of India.

APPENDIX II

THE FABULOUS RACES OF INDIA

1. *The Pygmies.* Called Pygmies by Ktesias, Τρισπάθιμοι by Megasthenes. The legend arose from the small, dwarf-like Mongolians of Nepal and Bhotan, called Kirrhadii by the *Periplus* and Ptolemy and *Kirāta* in Sanskrit. The Pygmies of Homer are Ethiopian, but Ethiopia and India were supposed to be connected. Referring to the fights between Cranes and Pygmies, Lassen recalls the term *Kirātāśin* (devourer of Kirāta) applied to Garuḍa, the vulture of Vishṇu.

2. **'Αμύκτηρες.** The noseless men, described by Megasthenes as eating carrion and dying young. Again we have the snub-nosed Mongolian. Παμφάγος is Skt. *sarva-bhaksha.*

3. **'Ενωτοκοῖται.** Men who sleep on their ears[1]. A literal translation of the Skt. *karṇaprāvaraṇa.* The Indians had many

[1] The legend is as old as Skylax, who also told the story of the one-eyed men, and many of the other legends here enumerated. Skylax called them 'Ωτόκλινοι. For the whole

such names for the aborigines, who hung weights to their ears and enlarged them to a great size by this and other means.

4. Ἀντίποδες or Ὀπισθοδάκτυλοι. The men whose feet turned backwards. Mentioned by Megasthenes and Ktesias. Skt. *Paśchādaṅgulaja*.

5. Ὠκύποδες. A curious mistranslation of Skt. *Ekapāda*. The Μονόσκελοι, Μονόκωλοι and Σκιάποδες of Ktesias[1], though the latter lived in Libya.

6. *The Hyperboreans*. This legend, like that of the Pygmies, is very old. It may belong to the primitive Indo-Aryan stock. They are the *Uttara-kuru* of the Indian epic, transliterated as Attakorae by later writers. Hekataeus wrote a pamphlet about them. Pindar places them north of the Danube[2].

7. Μονόμματοι. The Skt. *Ekāksha*. Mentioned by Megasthenes. Here again we have a legend which may be Indo-Aryan, as we find the Cyclops as early as the Odyssey.

8. Κυνοκέφαλοι and Κυνάμολγοι. The former are the Skt. *Śvamukha*. The latter may be aboriginal tribes who, like their successors to-day, may have kept packs of hunting dogs. The yellow Tibetan mastiffs of the Dards led to the legend of the gold-ants. These people occur in Ktesias and Megasthenes.

9. Ἄστομοι. Mouthless men who live on smell. The Indian equivalent has not been traced.

(Pliny's "Satyrs," *N.H.* VII. 2, are apes. His Στρουθόποδες, women—not men—with 'sparrow feet,' must be the Chinese. The early age of marriage and child-bearing in India gave rise to stories of women who conceive at five years old. The jungle-folk called Choromandae, who have no language, etc., are merely aboriginal tribes.)

subject, see Strabo, *Geog.* XV. I. 57, and McCrindle's learned note, *Ancient India*, p. 57.

[1] *Apud* Pliny, *N.H.* VII. 2. The story of the Σκιάποδες is as old as Hekataeus.

[2] The Πανδορή and Μακρόβιοι of Ktesias, and the Μάνδοι (? Πάνδοι) of Megasthenes belong to the same class.

APPENDIX III

THE ACCURACY OF MEGASTHENES

In view of Strabo's attacks upon the veracity of Megasthenes, it is curious to find that his account of the constitution of Chandragupta finds close confirmation in many details in a Hindu book on Politics, traditionally ascribed to Kauṭilya or Chāṇakya, the famous Brahmin minister of the Maurya Emperor. This work is the *Kauṭilīya Artha Śāstra.* In this book we find the king's palace described very much after the manner of Megasthenes, with its moats, ramparts and towers. The king is surrounded by a bodyguard of "women armed with bows," as Megasthenes says. (*Artha Śāstra,* II. 3.)

The *Artha Śāstra* describes the highly organized bureaucracy in terms very similar to those employed by Megasthenes, but in greater detail. Thus Megasthenes tells us that the district officers were in charge of the forests, temples, harbours, mines, roads, etc. He also describes the six Boards or *Panchāyats* who managed municipal affairs. Kauṭilya describes no less than fifteen officials or boards of officials who supervised municipal affairs. But the general duties assigned to them are nearly the same. Thus Kauṭilya describes a Superintendent of Commerce and a Superintendent of Warehouses, who between them managed the market, fixed the market-prices, regulated the trade in agricultural produce, levied the subsidies for provisioning the army, and collected the royal tithes on goods bought and sold. These were almost precisely the duties assigned to the first, fourth, fifth and sixth boards in the polity described by Megasthenes.

The *Artha Śāstra* mentions a Superintendent of Courtezans and of Public Gambling, two functions of the police department not occurring in Megasthenes. But Megasthenes tells us how the king's agents employed the courtezans to obtain information. This ancient profession was, as in most Indian polities, treated as a recognized trade, taxed, inspected, and utilized by Government. But on the whole, the two accounts supplement one another in a remarkable manner, though the *Artha Śāstra* increases our opinion of the severity of Chandragupta's government. The people were supervised and taxed with relentless severity.

On one important point Kauṭilya supplies information which supplements Megasthenes very considerably. This is with regard to the Board of Shipping. The Port Commissioner supervised sea and river-traffic and ferries. Fishermen, merchants and travellers, were all subjected to taxation and the ferries were in the hands of the Government. The fords were guarded by pickets, who prevented suspects from entering or leaving. It was the duty of the Harbour Masters to assist ships in distress, and of those in charge of the ferries to see that they were not used when the river was in a dangerous state.

(For a more detailed comparison, see *The Ancient Hindu Polity*, by N. N. Law (Longmans, 1914), especially pp. xxxv—xlv, Introduction. For text, see R. Shāma Śāstri's Edition, Mysore, 1909.)

[Since the above chapter was written, an article by Dr D. B. Spooner has appeared in *J.R.A.S.* 1915, p. 63. The author, who is in charge of the excavations at Pāṭaliputra, shews that the Persian element therein is far more extensive than is commonly supposed. The palace and other buildings are modelled on the palace of Darius at Persepolis, and seem to have been the work of Persian masons. The caves at Barābar etc. (Hiuen Tsiang's "stone-chambers") are copied from the Royal Tombs of the Persian kings. Asura Maya, the demon builder of the *Mahābhārata* (see Hopkins, *Great Epic of India*, p. 391), is the demon who according to Hiuen Tsiang built Aśoka's palace, and is no other than Ahura Mazda of Persia, by whose grace Xerxes built his palace (Curzon, *Persia*, II. p. 156).]

CHAPTER IV

GREEK AND SEMI-GREEK DYNASTIES OF THE PANJĀB

"The grete Emetreus, the king of Inde."

Knight's Tale, 2156.

THE ancient city of Baktra (*Bākhtri* or *Bākhdhi* in old Persian, the modern Balkh), like Constantinople or Alexandria, was destined by its geographical position to play a leading part in the history of the world. On the landward side, it was the key to India. At its gates converged almost all the great trade-routes of central Asia. First, there were the famous "three roads to Baktria[1]," running through Afghanistan and converging at Balkh. Then there was the road through Kashgar to the Stone Tower of Sarikol, by which the silk-traders brought their goods. Lastly, there were the two great highways to the West, the waterway of the Oxus, and the caravan road through Parthia to Antioch.

Balkh had been, for countless years, a Skythian settlement before the coming of the Iranians.

[1] ἡ εἰς Βακτριανὴν τρίοδος. Strabo, xv. 2. 8. See Bunbury, *Hist. Anc. Geog.* pp. 486–7.

After their advent, it became the capital of eastern Irān, separated from the rest of the Persian Empire by the vast Karmanian Desert, and never perfectly subdued. It became a fixed policy on the part of the Persian kings to leave the satrapy of Baktria in a state of practical independence, as it formed an outpost against the ever-growing menace of the Skythian hordes beyond the Oxus. Baktra was famous in Persian literature as the centre of the worship of Anahid, probably a Skythian goddess originally, who had there a great temple. Baktra fell, like the rest of Persia, before the invincible arms of Alexander, and formed a natural base for his invasion of India. Of the far-reaching projects of Alexander, his colonies in the Indus valley, and their fate, we have already spoken. Meanwhile Baktria, which had been made an important Macedonian settlement, became a part of the Syrian Empire, until its ruler, a certain Diodotus, took advantage of the incessant wars which distracted the king's attention to declare himself an independent sovereign. Parthia quickly followed suit. This must have been about 250 B.C., or a little later. Baktria finally extorted her independence in 208 B.C., when Antiochus III, after an unsuccessful siege of the capital, acknowledged the claims of Euthydemus, the Baktrian ruler, and gave him a Seleukid princess in marriage.

Meanwhile, the great Empire of the Mauryas was slowly breaking up. A succession of weak monarchs followed the death of Aśoka in 231 B.C., and it is not surprising that the Baktrians began to turn their attention to the rich plains which lay beyond the Paropamisus. There were probably already settled there considerable colonies of Yavanas, descendants of the Greek soldiers who preferred staying in India to participating in the evacuation of Eudamus in 317 B.C. At any rate, between 190 and 180 B.C., Demetrius, the son and successor of Euthydemus, conquered Ariana, crossed the Paropamisus, and subdued not only Pattalene or Sind, but also Surāshṭra,—the Kathiāwār and Surāt districts—and an obscure province which Strabo calls Sigertis[1]. At the same time, he extended the Baktrian Empire "to the Seres and Phrynoi." His object in both these undertakings was no doubt commercial. He pushed the limits of his realm to the edge of the Pamirs in order to control the silk-routes ; and by conquering Sind and Kathiāwār, he obtained an outlet to the sea by the great waterway of the Indus. Demetrius, apparently, made his Indian territories into a separate province. Its capital was Euthydemeia, the new name which he bestowed, in memory of his father, upon the ancient city of Sāgala[2]. Other towns which he built were

[1] *Δημήτριος ὁ Εὐθυδήμου υἱὸς τοῦ Βακτρίων βασιλέως οὐ μόνον δὲ τὴν Πατταληνὴν κατέσχεν ἀλλὰ καὶ τῆς ἄλλης παραλίας τήν τε Σαραόστου* (MSS. *τεσσαριόστου*) *καλουμένην καὶ τὴν Σιγερτίδος βασιλείαν.* Strabo, *Geog.* XI. II. I.

[2] *Σάγαλα ἡ καὶ Εὐθυδημεία*, says Ptolemy. It is probably Siālkot. See McCrindle, *Ancient India*, p. 37; V. A. Smith, *Anc. Hist. Ind.* p. 65 note.

Demetria in Sind and another town of the same name in Arachosia. He probably absorbed the remains of the older Greek principalities[1], whose capital, Alexandria-on-Indus, "Alasanda of the Yonas," was famous enough to find mention in the chronicles of the remote island of Ceylon. The fine coins struck by Demetrius illustrate very appropriately the events of his reign. In some, he wears upon his head a wonderful elephant-headed helmet, appropriate to the conqueror of India[2]. Another type[3], issued no doubt for circulation in his Indian domains, is the square type, bearing an inscription in Kharoshṭhī, the script then almost exclusively used in the North-West Frontier. A third type represents the king in extreme old age. On the reverse stands Anahid, the goddess of Baktra, with her starry crown[4]. It was in his old age that the great conqueror was defeated by a rival named

[1] Or are we to attribute this to Eukratides? Eukratides restrikes the coins of Apollodotus, and it may be supposed that Apollodotus was an indigenous "Yavana" prince and not a Baktrian. His coins are of a type all their own (Gardner, IX. 8–13). Another explanation is, of course, that Apollodotus was a prince of the House of Euthydemus, who reigned at Kāpiśa, and was conquered by Eukratides along with Demetrius and other members of the family. His coins are certainly associated with those of Menander. But there may be two princes of the same name.

[2] Gardner, *Cat. of Greek and Indo-Scythic Coins in the B.M.* II. 9–12.

[3] *Ibid.* XXX. 3.

[4] *Ibid.* III. 1. For the crown, see Zend Avesta in *S.B.E.* II. 82.

Eukratides, perhaps his grandson[1], who raised a rebellion against him during his absence[2]. Though Demetrius had an army of sixty thousand men, and his opponent's forces dwindled down to three hundred followers, Eukratides managed, after a blockade of five months, to cut his way out to safety and finally to depose Demetrius[3]. But the way of transgressors is hard, for Eukratides was finally slain, on his return from India, by his own son, who declared him to be "a public enemy and not a parent," and driving his chariot through his father's blood, ordered the body to be left unburied where it had fallen[4].

It is difficult to decide whether the parricide was Apollodotus II or Heliokles. Apollodotus II (it is usually supposed that there were two princes of the name), however, places the epithets Φιλοπάτωρ καὶ Σωτήρ on his coins, and the title would be somewhat incongruous under the circumstances. We are, therefore, driven to suppose that the murderer was Heliokles[5]. This was about 156 B.C.

[1] See the Author's *Baktria* (Probsthain, 1912), pp. 155–6.

[2] *Epit.* XLI. 6. "Multa tamen Eukratides bella magna virtute gessit quibus attritus cum obsidionem Demetrii regis Indorum pateretur cum CCC militibus LX milia hostium assiduis eruptionibus vicit. Quinto itaque mense liberatus Indiam in potestatem redegit."

[3] Date *c.* 174 B.C. Justin says that both Mithradates and Eukratides came to the throne about the same time. (*Epit.* XLI. 6. I.)

[4] Justin, *ibid.*

[5] See, however, Cunningham, *Num. Chron.* 1869, p. 241; Rapson, *J.R.A.S.* 1905, p. 783; Tarn, "Hellenism in Baktria," *J.H.S.* 1902, p. 272.

Eukratides was, if we may judge from his coins, a proud, determined man. One of these, a triumph of the coiner's art, represents him as wearing the *Kausia*[1] or sun hat. On the reverse are the charging Dioskuri[2].

The murder of Eukratides struck a fatal blow to the fortunes of Baktria. The country was beset by enemies. On the one side was Parthia, her ancient and inveterate rival. Under Mithradates I, she had already inflicted one serious reverse on Baktria, and had recaptured two outlying provinces[3]. On the other side, a still graver menace presented itself. The dangers of a Skythian invasion from across the Oxus had long threatened Baktria. Antiochus III had been induced to spare the town chiefly because, if it fell, "the Hellenic world would obviously be soon overrun by the barbarians[4]." The cause of the new invasion which now promised to inundate the country south of the Oxus was

[1] καυσία from καίω, the modern *solar topi*.

[2] Gard. V. 7. The coins of Demetrius, Eukratides and Antimachus are among the finest of the ancient world. It is impossible to account for this outburst of art in a remote corner of the Hellenic world. But the most artistic Greek nations were not the most skilful coiners, *e.g.* the coins of Athens are by no means remarkable and do not compare with those of Sicily.

[3] τὴν Ἀσπιώνην καὶ τὴν Τουρίουαν ἀφῄρηντο Εὐκρατίδην οἱ Παρθυαῖοι. Strabo, XI. 11. Mithradates imitates the coins of Demetrius and Eukratides, and Orosius has a tale that he invaded India as far as the Indus.

[4] ἐκβαρβαρωθήσεσθαι τὴν Ἑλλάδα ὁμολογουμένως. Polybius, XI. 34.

primarily a migration, from central Asia, of the great nomad tribe of the Yueh-chi, who, about 165 B.C., had been driven out of their pasture-lands, and had moved southwards, pressing before them in their turn the Sakae or Skythian tribes who lay on the borders of Sogdiana. The first omens of the coming trouble appeared in Parthia. A body of Skythian mercenaries, who, driven out of their native country by the advance of the tribes from central Asia, had enlisted in the service of Parthia, rebelled. A war followed, in which the Parthian monarch Artabanus was killed by a poisoned arrow[1]. Parthia, however, managed to beat back the invaders. It was otherwise with the Baktrians. Having dissipated their strength in various ambitious schemes, the Baktrian monarchs, exhausted by wars with the Parthians, Indians, and Sakae, were literally "drained of their life-blood" as Justin says, and unable to offer an effective resistance[2]. At first the Sakae contented themselves with occupying Sogdiana: finally, however, they pushed across the Oxus, and Heliokles and his followers were compelled to seek refuge in their domains across the Hindu Kush, and abandon Baktria to the invaders.

[1] Justin, XLII. 1, 2.

[2] Baktriani per varia bella jactati non regnum tantum, verum etiam libertatem amiserunt: siquidem Sogdianorum et Drangianorum Indorumque bellis fatigati ad postremum ab invalidioribus Parthis velut exsangues oppressi sunt. Justin, XLI. 6.

The Greek kingdom south of the Hindu Kush, did not, however, long remain intact. Even Eukratides had found it impossible to govern his extensive dominions single-handed, and had delegated part of his powers to his son[1]. Of the petty princes who split up the Panjāb among them, we know nothing except what we like to infer from the coins which have been unearthed from time to time. Many of these are extraordinarily fine, but they shed little light upon their strikers' history. If we may rely at all upon similarity of types and legends[2], we may infer that some of these princelets belonged to the house of Eukratides, and others to that of Euthydemus. About others we are quite uncertain. Thus we know that Agathokles and Antimachus claim descent from Euthydemus and Diodotus respectively[3]. Plato's coin is dated 165 B.C.[4], which makes him an early contemporary, probably a viceroy, of Eukratides. Apollodotus II, Strato, and Menander, employ the figure of Athene hurling the bolt, which first appears on the coins of Euthydemus. Hence we infer that they belong to his family. Heliokles, supposed to be the son and murderer of Eukratides, restrikes the coins of Strato, probably because he

[1] Eukratides a filio, *quem socium regni fecerat*, interficitur. Justin, XLI. 6.

[2] This is, of course, a most untrustworthy guide.

[3] Gardner, p. xxviii, Introd.

[4] He also wears on his helmet the bull's ear and horn of Eukratides. Gardner, VI. 11.

conquered territory belonging to the rival house. Antialkidas, on the other hand, restrikes coins of Eukratides. Diomedes[1] reproduces in a barbarous fashion the charging Dioskuri of Eukratides; hence we may suppose that he is a scion of that house. These problems, however, belong to the province of the numismatist rather than the historian, and these petty rulers are unknown to us except for their coins. About forty of them divided Sind and the Panjāb between them during the two centuries before and after the birth of Christ, and the epithet "fiercely fighting," applied to them by the Hindu writers, indicates fairly correctly, no doubt, the extent of their achievements. The "fierce fighting" was, doubtless between the rival houses. At first the family of Eukratides was successful. Eukratides beat Apollodotus II, and wrested from him the Kāpiśa district; Heliokles won territories from Strato. But with Antialkidas and Menander the tide turned in favour of the house of Euthydemus, though the family of Eukratides retained the Gandhāra and Kābul districts till the coming of the Sakae.

Only one of these monarchs achieved any real greatness. This was king Menander, or Milinda as he is called by the Buddhist writers, of whose career some details have been preserved in a Buddhist treatise, the *Milinda Pañha*, and in passages of Strabo and Plutarch. To him, too, we should very probably attribute the remarkable

[1] Gardner, VIII. 12.

Greek invasion of the Ganges Valley which penetrated almost to the walls of Pāṭaliputra itself, and which is mentioned by more than one Indian writer[1]. According to the *Milinda Pañha*[2], Menander was born, probably soon after the conquest of the Panjāb by Demetrius, perhaps about 180 B.C., in a village called Kalasi, on the island of Alasanda. This was no doubt an island at the confluence of the Indus and Akesines, which took its name from the adjacent town of Alexandria-on-Indus, the modern Ucch. His father may have been a viceroy, probably a relation, of Demetrius, left in charge of this important post. Strabo, who couples together, on the authority of Apollodorus of Artemita[3], the names of Demetrius and Menander, says that both monarchs made themselves masters of the Panjāb, Sind, and the Kathiāwār coast. Menander ascended the throne of Sāgala, which probably retained the position of the premier state or capital of the Greek principalities, about 155 B.C. It was about this time, no doubt, that his conversion to Buddhism took place[4]. Buddhism,

[1] This is usually taken for granted by writers, but is by no means *proved*.

[2] Trans. Rhys Davids in *S.B.E.* vol. XXXV.

[3] *Geog.* XI. II. I (quoted above). Many of Menander's coins bear the figure of Herakles or an elephant, both devices found also on the coins of Demetrius. Compare the coins of Menander in Gardner, XII, with those of Eukratides in Gardner, III. 2.

[4] There is no reason to doubt Menander's conversion, though the evidence of the coins is inconclusive. We know

which had been made, thanks to the efforts of Aśoka, the official religion of northern India, appealed especially to the casteless foreigners of the Indus valley. In the Middle Land, with the collapse of the Maurya dynasty, Brahminism was gradually beginning to reassert itself, though it encountered set-backs when foreign kings like Kanishka or Menander wielded a temporary supremacy over India.

Of the capital as it was in the time of Menander, the author of the *Milinda Pañha* gives us a fascinating description, which may not be entirely fanciful :

> " There is, in the country of the Yonakas, a great centre of trade, a city that is called Sāgala, situated in a delightful country, well-watered and hilly, abounding in parks and gardens and groves and lakes and tanks, a paradise of rivers and mountains and woods. Wise architects have laid it out, and its people know of no oppression, *since all their enemies and adversaries have been put down*[1]. Brave is its defence, with many and various strong towers and ramparts with superb gates and entrance archways, and with the royal citadel in its midst, white-walled and deeply-moated. Well laid-out are its streets, squares, cross-roads, and market-places. Well-displayed are the innumerable sorts of costly merchandise with which its shops are filled[2]. It is richly

from cave inscriptions that " Yonas " often adopted Buddhism as their creed.

[1] Does this refer to Menander's reduction of his Greek and Śaka rivals ?

[2] Menander had access to the sea on the one hand and the Seres on the other. See the quotation from Strabo given above.

adorned with hundreds of alms halls of various kinds, and splendid with hundreds of thousands of magnificent mansions which rise aloft like the peaks of the Himalayas. Its streets are filled with elephants, horses, carriages, and foot-passengers and crowded by men of all sorts and conditions,—Brahmins, nobles, artificers and servants. They resound with cries of welcome to teachers of every creed, and the city is the resort of leading men of each of the different sects. Shops are there for the sale of Benares muslin, of Kotumbara stuffs, and of other cloths of various kinds; and sweet odours are exhaled from the bazaars where all sorts of flowers and perfumes are tastefully set out. Jewels are there in plenty and guilds of traders in all sorts of finery display their goods in the bazaars which face all quarters of the sky."

Menander was not content, however, with the conquest of the Panjāb. He aimed at nothing less than the Empire of all northern India, the position of *Chakravarti*, attained by his great predecessor, Chandragupta. Perhaps his object was partly religious. He may have hoped to restore the *Dharma* to its old dominant position in Pāṭaliputra from which it had been ousted by the Śunga kings. Of his invasion of Magadha, echoes are found in contemporary Hindu literature[1]. Menander's first move was against the frontier towns of Maghada. He besieged Mathurā, Madhyamikā near Chitor, and Sāketa in Oude.

[1] As already pointed out, it is highly probable, but not absolutely certain, that the Yavana invasion here referred to was conducted by Menander. But the passage of Strabo, quoted below, shews that Menander *did* invade Magadha, and we have no records of *another* such Baktrian invasion.

"The Yavana was besieging Sāketa: the Yavana was besieging Madhyamikā," are examples given by the contemporary grammarian Patañjali of the imperfect tense, which indicates an event which has recently taken place, and is still fresh in men's memories. About this time the aged Pushyamitra, who had usurped the throne of the last of the Mauryas in 184 B.C., was contemplating offering the ancient Brahminical sacrifice of *Aśvamedha*, to celebrate his ascendancy over his neighbours. He received an unexpected check. On the banks of the Sindhu[1] river, the sacred horse and its bodyguard, under the command of the young Crown Prince Agnimitra, were attacked by a party of Yavana horsemen (perhaps a detachment of the army besieging Madhyamikā), and all but carried off[2]. Nor did Menander stop here. Pressing on, he began to threaten Pāṭaliputra itself, to the great alarm of the inhabitants. "When the viciously valiant Yavanas," says the author of the *Gārgī Saṃhitā*, "after reducing Sāketa, the Pañchāla country, and Mathurā, reach the royal residence of Pāṭaliputra, all the provinces will be in disorder." He penetrated, says Strabo, right to the Soanus[3]. But the fears

[1] Between Rājputāna and Bundelkhand. *Not*, of course, the Indus.

[2] See the drama called *Mālavikāgnimitra*, trans. Tawney, p. 78.

[3] πλείω ἔθνη κατεστρέψαντο ἢ Ἀλέξανδρος, καὶ μάλιστα ὁ Μένανδρος, εἴγε τὸν Ὕπασιν διέβη πρὸς ἕω καὶ μέχρι τοῦ Σοάνου προῆλθε (MSS Ὕπανιν . . . Ἰσάμου). Strabo, XI. II. I.

of contemporary writers were not realised, and Menander, as far as we know, never entered the ancient capital of Aśoka. "The fiercely-fighting Greeks," we are told, "did not stay long in Madhyadeśa: a cruel strife had broken out in their own country." Menander returned, and died soon after in the field. According to a Siamese version of the *Milinda Pañha* he was looked upon at the time of his death as an Arhat, a Buddhist saint of high degree. And so, says Plutarch, his subject states strove for his ashes, which they finally divided among them, and placed beneath great *dāgabas* in their own land, just as was done in the case of Gautama Buddha himself[1]. His coins are found in great quantities all over North-Western India, and as far south as Hamīrpur in the Jamna district. Over two centuries after Menander's death, the author of the *Periplus* found them still current at the port of Broach[2].

The war which recalled Menander was probably a Śaka invasion. The Śaka tribes, pushed steadily southwards by the advance of the Yueh-chi, and

[1] Μενάνδρου δέ τινος ἐπιεικῶς βασιλεύσαντος καὶ ἀποθανόντος ἐπὶ στρατοπέδου, τὴν μὲν ἄλλην κηδείαν ἐποιήσαντο κατὰ τὸ κοινὸν αἱ πόλεις· περὶ δὲ τῶν λειψάνων αὐτοῦ καταστάντες εἰς ἀγῶνα, μόλις συνέβησαν, ὥστε νειμάμενοι μέρος ἴσον τῆς τέφρας ἀπελθεῖν καὶ γενέσθαι μνημεῖα παρὰ πᾶσι τοῦ ἀνδρός. *De Rep. Ger.* 21.

For Gautama's funeral, see *Mahāparinibbāna Sutta* in *S.B.E.* XI. 131.

[2] § 47. Μέχρι νῦν ἐν Βαρυγάζαις παλαιαὶ προχωροῦσι δραχμαί... ἐπίσημα τῶν μετ' Ἀλέξανδρον βεβασιλευκότων Ἀπολλοδότου καὶ Μενάνδρου.

hemmed in on the west by the Parthians, overflowed Baktria and crossed the Helmand river into the country still known as Sakastene or Seistān. Here they were joined by allied Parthian or Pahlava tribes, and made their way into India through the Bolān Pass. Entering the Panjāb, they quickly superseded the now decaying power of the Baktrian Greeks, excepting a small principality ruled over by members of the house of Eukratides, which still held out in the Kābul valley. The invaders set up two allied kingdoms. At Mathurā reigned the Śaka line which was founded by Moga or Maues, who was apparently reigning in 93 B.C. Among his successors was Azes, whose coins indicate that he ruled over a wide area. Under him were the satraps Liaka Kusūlaka and Pātika at Taxila, and Rājavula and Śodāsa at Mathurā[1]. These rulers restrike the coins of Demetrius, Eukratides, and Strato, whose territories they doubtless conquered. Meanwhile, a Parthian prince named Vonones set up a dynasty in Baluchistān and Khandahār, and the two families were finally united under the rule of the Parthian prince Gondophares in the first century A.D. Gondophares is interesting, as, according to a widely-spread legend, he and his followers were

[1] There is, of course, much argument on all these points, and the identity of Maues with Moa, and his date, are still under discussion. But a detailed account is here out of place. See V. A. Smith, *Ancient India*, ch. VII. The coins are barbarous imitations of debased Indian models, with Parthian titles like *βασιλεὺς βασιλέων*, Chhatrapa, etc.

converted to Christianity by the Apostle Thomas. At the same time, a Śaka chief of the Kshaharāta clan named Nahapāna gained some temporary successes against the Āndhra monarchs in the Northern Deccan, and struck some creditable imitations of Indo-Greek coins.

Lastly, about the last quarter of the first century B.C., the Yueh-chi, after conquering Baktria, descended upon India. The leading tribe, the Kushāns, had now gained the supremacy, and headed by the monarch Kujūla Kadphises, they invaded Kābul, and conquered the last of the Baktrian monarchs, Hermaeus, as the coins clearly indicate[1]. The Kushān kings finally, at a date which is still quite uncertain, conquered and superseded the Indo-Parthian dynasty, and under their monarch Kanishka, became the paramount power in India. The Kushāns had, no doubt, many Greek and semi-Greek subjects, and it is uncertain whether they employed Baktrian Greeks or outsiders to execute the remarkable Gandhāra sculptures which are the most striking relic of their period which we possess[2]. Their coins are singularly interesting. They bear traces of imitation of both Baktrian and Roman models, but they also shew a great deal of artistic originality and power of realistic portraiture. The Greek element in India was now rapidly absorbed. Yavanas appear among the pious donors in the Buddhist

[1] Gard. XXV. 1–3.

[2] For a fuller discussion of this point, see ch. VII.

INDO-GREEK AND INDIAN COINS

1. Gold double daric, struck in the Panjāb in the time of the Persian occupation. Probably belongs to Darius Codomannus, 337 B.C. (Rapson, *Indian Coins*, I. 5.)

2. Athenian *owl*, probably struck in India in imitation of Athenian coinage. (*Ibid.* I. 6.)

3. Coin of Sophytes (*Saubhūti*), king of the Salt Range at the time of Alexander's invasion. (*Ibid.* I. 8.)

4. Coin of Eukratides, king of Baktria, Kābul, and the Panjāb (*c.* 175 B.C.). (Gardner, *B.M. Cat.* V. 8.)

5. Coin of Demetrius, king of Baktria, Kābul, and the Panjāb (*c.* 190 B.C.). (*Ibid.* II. 9.)

6. Coin of Menander, Greek king of the Panjāb (Sākala) (*c.* 165 B.C.). (*Ibid.* XI. 7.)

7. Coin of Maues, Śaka ruler in the Panjāb, who conquered the territories of Demetrius (?*c.* 21 A.D.). (*Ibid.* XXI. I.)

8. Coin of Nahapāna, Kshaharāta chieftaiṇ who ruled in the northern Deccan and Gujarat (*c.* 100 A.D.). (Rapson, *op. cit.* III. I.)

9. Coin of Kanishka, the greatest of the Kushan kings, who ruled at Peshāwar. His date is disputed, perhaps *c.* 120 A.D. (Gardner, *op. cit.* XXVI. I.)

10. Coin of Samudragupta, Gupta Emperor of Northern India, 326 A.D. (Allen, *B.M. Cat.* V. I.)

11. Coin of Puḷumavi, Āndhra king of the Deccan, 1st century A.D. (Rapson, *Āndhra Cat.* V. 89.)

12. Coin of Kanishka, with standing figure of Buddha and Greek inscription BOΔΔO. (Gardner, *op. cit.* XXVI. 8.)

To face coin plate

Indo-Greek and Indian Coins

caves of Kārla and Nāsik, but they bear Indian titles, and were doubtless Greek in little more than name. Perhaps the latest reference to them occurs in the inscription of the Āndhra queen Bālaśrī, 144 A.D., who boasts that she rooted the "Sakas, Yavanas and Pahlavas," out of the Deccan for ever[1].

APPENDIX

GREEK AND SEMI-GREEK RULERS IN BAKTRIA AND THE PANJĀB

(This list is entirely conjectural. Semi-Greek includes all kings minting coins which have Greek inscriptions. The various theories on this vexed subject may be found in Gardner's *Catalogue of Greek and Indo-Scythian Coins in the B.M.*, V. A. Smith's *Early History of India*, Ch. VIII.–IX., Duff's *Chronology of India*, Barnett's Chronology in *Antiquities of India*, pp. 36–94, and articles in the *J.R.A.S.* and other Oriental Journals.)

I. Greek Kings of Baktria

Diodotus I, 250 B.C. Diodotus II, 245 B.C.
Euthydemus I, 230 B.C.

II. Greek Kings of Baktria and Sāgala

Demetrius, 200 B.C. Eukratides, 165 B.C.
Heliokles, 156 B.C.

[1] Kārla Inscr. No. 17 (*Archaeological Survey of Western India*, ed. Bühler, IV. 109.) Her son Gautamīputra actually carried this out.

III. Greek Kings of Sāgala and other principalities in N.W. India

(*a*) *Family of Euthydemus*

Antimachus	Pantaleon
Agathocles	Euthydemus II
Philoxenus	Strato I and II and Agathokleia
Menander	Antialkidas
Apollodotus II	Menander

(*b*) *Family of Eukratides*

Plato (contemporary)	Zoilus
Lysias	Antimachus
Hippostratus	Philoxenus
Pantaleon	Archebius
Diomedes	Hermaeus (last Greek ruler, deposed about 25 B.C.)

(*c*) *Uncertain*

Apollophanes	Hippostratus
Epander	Epander
Amyntas	Telephus
Artemidorus	Peukelaus
Nikias	Zoilus

IV. Śaka and Indo-Parthian

(*a*) *Śaka Princes* (*House of Maues*)

Maues c. 93 B.C.[1] Azes I and II

Azilises

[1] This is quite uncertain. Fleet says 21 A.D.

(*b*) *Indo-Parthian Princes* (*House of Vonones*)

Vonones
Spalirises (brother of Vonones)
Gondophares (1st cent. A.D., unites Śakas and Parthians)
Orthagnes
Arsakes
Pakores
Sandbares

(*c*) *Satraps subordinate to Maues*

(1) Liaka, Pātika } Satraps of Taxila
(2) Rājavula, Sodāsa } Satraps of Mathurā

(*d*) *Kshaharāta satraps*

Bhumaka Nahapāna

V. Kushān Kings

Kujūla Kadphises, c. 25 B.C.
Wima Kadphises
Kanishka 78 A.D.[1]
Huvishka
Vāsudeva

[1] This would be Kanishka's date if he is regarded as the founder of the Śaka era. Fleet, Barnett and others, apparently consider Kanishka as the *first* of the Kushān line, and identify his accession with the commencement of the Vikramāditya era, *i.e.* 58 B.C.

CHAPTER V

THE PTOLEMIES

We now turn to another aspect of Indian intercourse with the West—the trade with Egypt. The Hellenization of Egypt was one of the most important results of Alexander's conquests, for Egypt became the true centre of Greek culture in the Hellenistic world, after Athens had dwindled into insignificance. The port of Alexandria was admirably chosen as the site of a great town. Not only does it tap the vast resources of the opulent country which lies along the banks of that great waterway, the Nile, but it enjoys an almost ideal situation as an emporium for trade between Europe and the East. It is on the Mediterranean, yet within easy distance of the head of the Red Sea. Alexandria is still an undying monument to the imperial genius of the great Macedonian whose name it bears. Like Constantinople, Baktra, and some other towns, it stands at the meeting-place of nations, in a spot destined by the nature of things to play a great part in the history of the world.

Many circumstances concurred, in the two centuries before Christ, to make the Red Sea route the most popular trade-route with the East. The anarchy reigning in Syria, and the growth of the hostile empire of Parthia, diverted the commerce from the more northerly routes. These were rendered still more unsafe by the irruption of the Skythian tribes from beyond the Oxus into Baktria. Another circumstance which tended to make Alexandria the metropolis of the Eastern Mediterranean, and which had effectually crippled her only possible rival, was the sack by Alexander of the great city of Tyre.

The ancient port of Naukratis had been comparatively neglected in favour of Tyre by the Oriental traders, owing to the long and perilous desert-journey between the Nile and the Red Sea. For the greater part of the year it was so intensely hot that the caravans had to move at night, guiding themselves across the trackless sands by means of stars, and carrying their own water-supply, like mariners, says Strabo[1]. Early attempts to remedy this by means of a canal between the two waterways had been made from time to time. The first attempt of this kind was due to a Sesostris of the twentieth century B.C. Pharaoh Necho and Darius the Great[2], and finally Ptolemy Philadelphus (285–246 B.C.), revived the idea. The latter built a large port at Arsinoe, the modern Suez, for the purpose. Owing, however, to the dangerous nature of the navigation of the Heroopolite Gulf, with its shoals

[1] *Geog.* XVII. I. 45. [2] Herod. II. 158.

and treacherous winds and currents, the scheme had finally to be abandoned[1], and it was left to the genius of De Lesseps in our own times to carry it into effect. Merchants preferred to take their goods to Aelana[2], the ancient Ezion Geber, whence they were transported to the great emporium of Petra, and thence to the Levantine ports. Ptolemy now reverted to the old idea of a port on the Egyptian coast of the Red Sea, connected with the Nile by a desert-road furnished with convenient oases. The spot chosen had a fine natural harbour, and was two hundred and fifty-eight miles from the trading station of Koptos (Koft), on the bend of the river[3]. Merchandise was to be conveyed overland to Koft, and floated down-stream to Alexandria. The port which was built at the chosen site was named Berenike[4], after the king's mother. A desert-road, furnished with eight *Hydreumata* or watering-places, connected Koft and Berenike. The first, says Pliny[5], was twenty-two miles from Koptos; the next, a day's journey (about twenty miles); the third, ninety-five

[1] Strabo, *Geog.* XVI. 4. 6.

[2] Or rather, to Leuke Kome, further down the coast and safer for ships. From Leuke Kome goods went through Petra to Rhinokolura (El Arish), a penal settlement on the Egyptian border of Palestine, and thence to Egypt. Strabo, *Geog.* XVI. 4. 24.

[3] Koft (Lat. 26° N.) is now a mile from the river bank.

[4] 23° 55′ N. 35° 34′ E. The remains of the town may still be seen.

[5] *N.H.* VI. 26.

miles from the base; the fourth, on a hill, at an uncertain distance; the fifth (the Apollo Hydreuma) one hundred and eighty-four miles; the sixth, on a mountain; the seventh, the New Hydreuma, was two hundred and thirty miles from the base; the last, seven miles further on, had a caravanserai, for two thousand persons and a guard. A single day's journey from here brought the merchant to the sea. The journey took eleven or twelve days, even under the most favourable conditions. In 274 B.C., a further improvement was made. Philadelphus built another port at Myos Hormos[1], (Mussel Harbour) one hundred and eighty miles north of Berenike, and five days nearer Koptos. Myos Hormos, situated in the bay of Ras abn Somer, near the Jifātin Islands, is a much safer harbour than Berenike, which had awkward shoals and was exposed to the wind[2]. Myos Hormos was thus almost an ideal port and became the great trading centre for the East Indian trade, quickly eclipsing all its rivals[3]. Further down the coast were Adulis (the modern Massowa) and Ptolemais Epitherōn (Ptolemais of the Hunts), a great rendezvous of the elephant-hunters from Nubia. Besides the value of their ivory, elephants had been in great requisition for military purposes, ever since the five hundred presented by Chandragupta to Seleukus Nikator had taken a prominent

[1] 27° 12′ N. 33° 55′ E.

[2] Strabo, *Geog.* XVI. 4. 6.

[3] *Ibid.* 24.

part in the battle of Ipsus[1]. They had been employed by Porus against Alexander and were later used by Pyrrhus and Hannibal against the Romans. The tactical value of these unwieldy beasts against well-disciplined troops is not great, and they quickly fell into disrepute in European warfare. They continued, however, to form one of the four traditional "arms" of the Indian army and were freely used as late as the days of the Moghal Empire. Ptolemais of the Hunts was probably not far from Port Sudan, and may then, as now, have been linked with the Nile by a road running to Berbera. The port of Adulis was chiefly famous for the inscription, preserved for us by Kosmas Indikopleustes[2], which recites the conquests of Ptolemy Euergetes (247–233 B.C.). It was the natural port for Abyssinia and the Sudan.

The knowledge possessed about India by the Alexandrian Greeks was chiefly due to Eratosthenes, the learned President of the Library from 240–196 B.C., though some facts must have been made known before this by Dionysius, who had been sent to India, says Pliny, in the reign of Philadelphus on an embassy, and published details about the forces of the Indian nations on his return. His account of India, contained in the third book of his *Geography*, was considered by

[1] Antiochus III was given one hundred and fifty by Subhāgasena. Polybius, XI. 34. Dittenberger, *Orientis Graeci Inscriptiones Selectae*, 54.

[2] Bunbury, *Anc. Geog.* II, 609.

Strabo[1] to be of the greatest value, superior to that of Megasthenes. Eratosthenes depended for his information upon the data supplied by Patrokles, an officer who held an important command over the eastern provinces of the Syrian Empire under Seleukus Nikator and Antiochus I. He appears to have used the opportunities he thus enjoyed in an admirable manner, and to have collected much invaluable information. Eratosthenes goes a good deal further than his contemporaries in his knowledge of the general configuration of India, which he describes as a rhomboid, its four sides being composed of the Indus, the Himālayas, and the shores of the Eastern and Southern Oceans respectively[2]. He knows of the Royal Road to Pāṭaliputra and of the mouth of the Ganges. He has heard of the "summer rains," brought by the Etesian winds, and watering the flax, rice, millet, and other crops. He calls the people of Southern India the Koniaki (a reminiscence of Cape Kory), and he has heard of Ceylon and its numerous elephants[3].

At this time, however, there was little *direct* trade with India. Athenaeus tells us that in the processions of Ptolemy Philadelphus were to be seen Indian women, Indian hunting dogs, and Indian cows, among other strange sights; also Indian spices carried on camels. The same

[1] Strabo, *Geog.* XV. 10.

[2] Strabo, I. I. 22 and XV. II. Arrian, *Indika,* III. See Cunningham, *Anc. Geog. of India,* p. I.

[3] Strabo, XV. 14.

authority tells us that Ptolemy Philopator's yacht had a saloon lined with Indian stone[1]. Agatharchides, the learned tutor of Ptolemy Soter II (116 B.C.) writes enthusiastically of the commercial enterprise of the Egyptian monarchs, and the wealth and number of the Red Sea ports. But his knowledge ends there. He speaks of Sokotra as "recently discovered," as if Alexandrian sailors had only just ventured outside the Straits of Bab-el-Mandeb, and then not far. In more than one place he indicates that merchandise was not brought direct from India, but carried to an intermediate port and there bought and shipped by the Alexandrian traders. For instance, in speaking of the great riches of Arabia Felix, he says it was partly due to the Indian traders who came in great numbers from Potana, the port founded by Alexander on the Indus. Potana is of course Pātala[2]: the very mistake shews how ignorant Agatharchides is of Indian matters. Evidently Indian goods were taken to Muza[3] or Aden, two ports at the mouth of the Red Sea, and there transhipped. Aden, called, from the country in which it lay, Arabia Felix or Eudaemon, was the great clearing-house of the East, just as Port Said is to-day. The author of the *Periplus*, writing of the early history of Aden, states this very clearly.

[1] *Deipnosophistes*, IV. 4–6, and V. 25, 39. And compare Q. Curtius, VIII. 9. [2] Bunbury, *Ancient Geography*, II. 59.

[3] Mocha, 13° 20′ N. 48° 20′ E. The neighbouring village is still called Mauza.

" It was called Eudaemon," says this writer, " because, in the early days of the city, when the direct voyage from India to Egypt was never made, and no one dared to sail from Egypt all the way to the ports on the other side of the Indian Ocean, the various nations met here, and it received cargoes from both, just as Alexandria is the emporium for traffic from Egypt and abroad to-day[1]." The port of Muza was " crowded with Arab ship-masters and sailors, and heaped with bales of merchandise ; for these Arabs carry on a trade with Barygaza, sending their own ships there[2]." Obviously, then, the trade between Alexandria and India in the days of the Ptolemies was mostly, if not entirely, indirect[3], and the Alexandrian Greeks knew little or nothing of the country from which the goods originally came. The information collected by Eratosthenes, for instance, was all second-hand ; it had been acquired from a Syrian officer and not from Egyptian traders. Eratosthenes had nothing to say of the voyage to India or of the intermediate ports on the Red Sea and Arabian coasts. There were, of course, important exceptions to this rule. Dionysius had found his way to India, and centuries ago the

[1] *Periplus Maris Erythraei*, § 26. [2] *Ibid.* § 21.

[3] The only evidence to the contrary consists in two mentions in Inscriptions (Dittenberger 186 and 190), of the office of Στρατηγὸς τῆς Ἰνδικῆς καὶ Ἐρυθρᾶς θαλάσσης. But nothing is known of his duties, which may have merely been those of a port-officer at the mouth of the Red Sea.

voyage had been accomplished by Skylax of Karyanda. Strabo's statement[1] that in the days of the Ptolemies "*very few* accomplished the voyage to India and brought home merchandise," seems to imply that *some* did. One of these, the famous explorer Eudoxus, actually made the voyage twice, and fortunately a brief account of his adventures[2] is preserved in a chapter of Strabo, taken, we are told, from the lost work of the Stoic philosopher Poseidonius.

Eudoxus was a native of Cyzicus. Having acquired a certain reputation as a geographer and ethnologist, he was sent by the authorities of his native city to undertake the exploration of the Nile. While in Egypt, however, his attention was diverted by a romantic incident. The coast-guards from the Red Sea brought to Alexandria an Indian whom they had found drifting in a boat, half dead with hunger and thirst. After he had learnt a little Greek, the Indian explained that he had set out from India with a ship's company; they had lost their bearings and drifted for months, till his companions had perished, one by one, of hunger; and at last, at the point of death, he had been picked up off the entrance to the Red Sea. He offered, if the government would provide a ship to take him back, to shew them the way to India. The offer was gladly accepted

[1] Πρότερον ἐπὶ τῶν Πτολεμαικῶν βασιλέων, ὀλίγων παντάπασι θαῤῥούντων πλεῖν καὶ τὸν Ἰνδικὸν ἐμπορεύεσθαι φόρτον. Strabo, *Geog.* II. 5. 12.

[2] *Ibid.* II. 3. 4.

by the monarch, Euergetes II[1], and Eudoxus accompanied the expedition. They took a supply of goods, reached India, and after exchanging their wares for Indian spices and gems, sailed home. Instead of rewarding them, Euergetes basely confiscated their cargo! He died, however, in 117 B.C. and the indomitable sailor obtained permission to try again, this time with a richer cargo. Again he reached the coast of India, but on his return voyage he was caught in a storm, and missing the entrance to the Red Sea, reached the African coast somewhere considerably south of Cape Gardafui. Here he conciliated the natives by presents, and received much kindness from them in return, for they gave him water and pilots for the homeward journey. He wrote down, like the scholar he was, several words of their language. But the strangest thing that happened there was the discovery of a ship's prow carved in the form of a horse. The natives declared that it belonged to a strange ship which came from the *west*[2]. Eudoxus took the prow back to Alexandria. Here he was again basely robbed[3], on the plea that he had misappropriated the ship's cargo. But some

[1] 146–117 B.C.

[2] This strange story of course is open to grave doubts. But it may be true.

[3] By Ptolemy Lathyrus, who was now reigning in place of his mother Cleopatra who had sent out the expedition (112 B.C.). Apparently the Indian treasures proved too much for the cupidity of the "Graeculus esuriens."

sailors declared that the prow was that of a Cadiz ship, and one even asserted that it was the actual prow of a vessel which had sailed away "beyond the river Lixus in Mauretania" and had never been heard of again. Eudoxus now shook the dust of Alexandria from off his feet, and sailed home. The information he had acquired presented two fascinating problems. Had the mysterious vessel whose prow he had found, really rounded Africa? And if so, was it possible to reach India by following this course? Eudoxus determined to try. Having realised his whole fortune, he fitted out a ship, with which he sailed to Italy, Marseilles, and Cadiz, collecting subscriptions for the great undertaking. Everywhere the project was hailed with enthusiasm, and Eudoxus was able to fit out at Cadiz a large vessel with two light boats for exploring the coast. Embarking doctors, artizans, bales of goods, and, strangely enough, "a supply of Spanish dancing girls," the expedition "set sail for India." Passing Gibraltar, they at first kept well out to sea; but the sailors grew frightened, and Eudoxus, against his better judgment, stood in shore. As he had feared, the large vessel ran aground, and had to be dismantled, a smaller boat being constructed out of her timbers. They went on and reached an Ethiopian tribe who, he thought, spoke a dialect similar to that which he had studied in East Africa. He was now compelled, owing to want of provisions, to return; but shortly afterwards he fitted out yet another expedition, and this time he intended to winter at one of the large, uninhabited and fertile islands he had observed on the way, probably the Canary Isles or Madeira [1], and sail on when the weather and wind permitted. For this purpose he took seeds and agricultural implements, so as to grow a fresh stock of provisions. Of the end of this brave mariner, who twice reached India and anticipated, in design at least, the projects of Vasco da Gama, we hear no more. From the silence which history observes with regard to his end, we may gather that he never reached home after rounding the Cape. The noteworthy thing about his career is the fact that he twice reached India and that he conceived the project of a voyage to that land by way of South Africa to be a feasible thing.

Of the intercourse between India and the Egypt of the Ptolemies, traces are few, because the trade between the two countries was mostly indirect. A unique inscription on the ruins of a shrine between Edfū and the ancient Berenike, records the visit of an Indian named Sophon [2].

[1] Like the "Fortunate Isles" to which Sertorius wanted to sail away, according to Plutarch's story (ch. 8, *Life of Sertorius*).

[2] Leipsius, *Denkmäler*, vol. VI, p. 81. It runs as follows:

Πανὶ Εὐόδῳ
καὶ Ὑπηκόῳ
Σόφων Ἰνδὸς
ὑπὲρ αὐτοῦ.

Dr Hultzsch speaks of finding a solitary silver coin of the days of Ptolemy Soter in the Bangalore bazaar[1]. The love-story, the progenitor of the modern novel, introduced to the West by Chares of Mitylene, may be perhaps considered an indirect product of Alexandrian influence, as it appears first in Alexandrian literature.

APPENDIX

THE PTOLEMIES

Ptolemy Soter I	321 B.C.
„ Philadelphus	285 „
„ Euergetes I	246 „
„ Philopator	221 „
„ Epiphanes	204 „
„ Philometor	181 „
„ Euergetes II	146 „
„ Soter II	117 „
„ Auletes	80 „
Cleopatra	51–30 B.C.

THE SELEUKIDS

Seleukus I	312 B.C.
Antiochus I (*Soter*)	281 „
Antiochus II (*Theos*)	260 „
Seleukus II (*Kallinikus*) ..	246 „
Seleukus III (*Soter*)	227 „
Antiochus III (*Megas*) ...	222 „
Seleukus IV (*Philopator*) ..	187 „
Antiochus IV (*Epiphanes*) .	175 „
Antiochus V (*Eupator*)	165 „
Demetrius (*Soter*)	163–150 B.C.

[1] *J.R.A.S.* 1904, p. 403.

CHAPTER VI

INDIA AND THE ROMAN EMPIRE

οὐ γάρ μοι βίος ἐστὶ μελαινάων ἐπὶ νηῶν,
οὐδέ μοι ἐμπορίη πατρώιος, οὐδ' ἐπὶ Γάγγην,
ἔρχομαι οἷά τε πολλοί....

IN the first centuries before and after Christ, when the Kushāns were establishing themselves among the ruins of the Baktrian and other semi-Greek principalities of North-Western India, great changes were taking place in the West. Rome was absorbing the remnants of the Empire of Alexander. Syria had already fallen: Egypt became a Roman province in 30 B.C. The dissensions of the civil war ended at Actium, after which Augustus settled down to organize and regulate his vast possessions. The effect of the *Pax Romana* upon trade was, of course, very marked. Piracy was put down, trade-routes secured, and the fashionable world of Rome, undistracted by conflict, began to demand, on an unprecedented scale, oriental luxuries of every kind. Silk from China, fine muslins from India, and jewels, especially beryls[1] and pearls, were

[1] The beryl, βήρυλλος from Skt. *vaiḍūrya,* is the much-prized aquamarine of the Romans. Only two beryl mines existed in S. India, at Padiyūr and Vaniyambādi, and they were a great source of wealth.

exported from eastern ports for personal adornment. Drugs, spices, and condiments, as well as costus, lycium and other cosmetics fetched high prices. Even greater was the demand for pepper, which sold in the days of Pliny at the price of 15 denarii a pound[1]. This seems extraordinary to us, but pepper remained one of the most highly-prized luxuries in the West, even in the Middle Ages. In the fifteenth century it sold at two shillings a pound,—about three pounds in its modern equivalent! Gibbon[2] tells us that among the ransom demanded by Alaric, was 3000 lb. of pepper. The Zamorin of Calicut correctly gauged European taste when he sent his famous letter to the King of Portugal by Vasco da Gama, saying that "In my land is an abundance of cinnamon, cloves, ginger, pepper and precious stones," and asking for specie in exchange. Pliny, who is fond of indulging in trite homilies on Roman extravagance, is right in complaining of the drain upon Roman finance caused by the Indian trade. India produced very little coinage (and what she did produce was mostly imitated from Greek and Roman coins), and her great gold-mines in Dardistān appear to have been practically worked out, probably by the exorbitant demands of her Persian and other early rulers. The specie received from Europe was absorbed as it is very largely to-day. The huge hoards of coins found in the Madras Presidency shew what

[1] *N.H.* XII. 14.
[2] *Decline and Fall*, III. 272.

became of the money. This is especially true of the first five Roman emperors, for, if we may judge from the Roman coins unearthed in India, the trade in Indian luxuries, which reached its height in the reign of Nero, began after this to decline, partly owing to civil war, but still more on account of the severer style of living encouraged by Vespasian and the Antonines[1]. Of the earlier emperors, 612 gold, and 1187 silver coins have been unearthed, exclusive of hoards variously described as "pots full" and "cooly loads." By far the greater part of these huge numbers belongs to the reigns of Augustus and Tiberius. Pliny[2] says that India, China, and Arabia, absorbed between them one hundred million sesterces per annum. This sum is calculated by Mommsen[3] to represent £1,100,000, of which nearly half went to India. The effect of this enormous drain on imperial finance must have been terribly serious. Roman coinage was, like English gold, the chief medium,—almost the sole medium—of international commerce. Indians had no coinage worth speaking of, and preferred to import specie. This was especially true of the south; the Kushān and Śaka monarchs imitated or restruck Roman coins. The well-known story of the Roman revenue collector, shipwrecked

[1] Sewell, *Roman Coins found in India* (*J.R.A.S.* 1904, p. 200 ff.).

[2] *N.H.* XII. 18. (41).

[3] *Provinces of the Roman Empire*, II. 300.

on the Ceylon coast and convincing the Sinhalese monarch of the superiority of his country by pointing to the purity, regularity and fine workmanship of her coins, is told by both Pliny[1] and Kosmas Indikopleustes[2]. "Thus it is," says the latter, "that with their money the trade of the world is carried on." One of the fashionable extravagances of the time was the consumption of huge quantities of spices at funerals. Even as early as the days of Sulla, we hear of two hundred and ten talents' weight being used at his obsequies. The climax was, of course, reached by Nero, who at the funeral of Poppoea, in 66 A.D., burnt more aromatics on her pyre than Arabia produced in a year[3]. Extravagance of this kind immensely stimulated the Indian trade, while it brought vast wealth to the inhabitants of Arabia Felix, and the cinnamon country (Ἡ Κιννναμωνόφορος) of the adjoining Somali coast.

One of the results of the increased intercourse with India was the appearance of several works bearing more or less directly upon the subject of Indian geography. Of these writers, the earliest is Strabo, an Asiatic Greek who lived in the reign of Augustus. A great traveller, Strabo had visited Armenia, and had accompanied his friend Aelius Gallus up the Nile. He had been to the port of Myos Hormos, and observed the great increase of trade with India; for he found

[1] *N.H.* VI. 22.

[2] *Christian Topography*, Bk. XI.

[3] *Ibid.* VII. 42.

that about one hundred and twenty merchantmen sailed to India (he does not say in what space of time, but perhaps he means in a single season), whereas scarcely anyone dared to make the direct voyage in the days of the Ptolemies[1]. In his own days a few bold sailors even made the mouth of the Ganges. But they were ignorant men, ill-qualified to describe what they had seen. Hence Strabo is driven to rely for his information about India upon previous writers[2]. His leading authority is Eratosthenes, the Alexandrian. He draws also largely upon Megasthenes (whom he unfairly censures), and on Aristobulus, Onesikritus, Nearchus, and other writers who took part in Alexander's campaign. Hence the India he describes is the India, not of his own day, but of the third and fourth centuries B.C.; and valuable and exhaustive though the fifteenth book of the *Geography* is, it throws little light upon India at the time of Augustus. Even with regard to the accounts of eye-witnesses, he says, there are many discrepancies, and most of the people who write about India do so from hearsay, having visited only isolated portions of the country. The same remarks apply to the *Indika* of Arrian, written about 150 B.C. A work of quite a different kind is the encyclopaedic *Natural History* of Pliny the Elder, completed in the year 77 A.D. two years before his death in the great eruption at Pompeii. The sixth book of this work contains

[1] Strabo, *Geog.* II. 5. 12. [2] *Ibid.* XV. 2.

a valuable description of Ceylon, drawn from the accounts of the official already mentioned (a freedman of Annius Plocamus) wrecked there in the reign of the Emperor Claudius. It also contains, besides dissertations on the geography of India drawn from various sources, a most interesting account of the voyage from Myos Hormos to the Indian coast, as made at the time. Other books contain exhaustive catalogues of Indian animals and minerals, and, above all, an invaluable list of Indian plants and drugs, of the greatest use in studying Indian exports of that nature.

About the time of Pliny's great work[1], an anonymous pamphlet entitled *Periplus Maris Erythraei* was published, probably at Alexandria. This little book is unique in the history of Greek geography, in so far as the writer describes the coasts of the Red Sea, Arabia, and Western India from his own experience and not at second-hand, as the other extant authorities do. This important work will receive detailed attention later. The last of the great geographers to write about India, if we except minor authorities and incidental references, is Ptolemy, who lived about 150 A.D. Unfortunately Ptolemy's *Guide to Geography* is mathematical rather than descriptive. His object is not to describe places, but to determine their latitude and longitude

[1] There are amazing discrepancies of opinion about the date of the *Periplus*. It is fairly certain, however, that it was written between 80 and 90 A.D. and nearer 80 than 90.

on the map, and his notices are occasional and brief. Later geographers (with the honourable exception of Kosmas Indikopleustes, one of the last writers of the fast-expiring ancient world), confine themselves to incidental statements about India, generally copied from Pliny, Strabo, and Ptolemy. The romances of Aelian and Philostratus are unworthy of serious notice.

The news of the accession of Augustus quickly reached India. Many Indian states sent embassies to congratulate him, an honour, as he remarks, never paid before to any Western prince[1]. The most striking of these was one sent by an important king, called, according to Strabo, Porus by some and Pandion by others[2]. If his name really was Pandion, he was one of the Pāṇḍya kings of Madurā, the most southerly of the three Tamil kingdoms. Porus, however (*Paurava*, a descendant of Puru) became a kind of generic name for an Indian king with the Greeks since the days of Alexander. It is tempting to identify this Porus with Kadphises the first, if it is possible to put the first of the Kushān monarchs so early[3]. The embassy sailed from Barygaza; it brought in its train a Buddhist monk, Zarmanochegas

[1] *Mon. Ancyranum*, 36.

[2] Strabo, *Geog.* XV. 4 & 73; Dion Cassius, LIV. 9. 58; Priaulx, *Indian Travel*, p. 64, and *Indian Embassies to Rome* (*J.R.A.S.* XIX. 294).

[3] Vincent Smith gives 45 A.D. as his date, but other authorities put him seventy years earlier.

(*Śramaṇāchārya*), who imitated the notorious Kalanos by burning himself on a pyre at Athens, and a letter written in Greek, describing Porus as "lord over six hundred kings." All this answers to the Kushān rather than the Tamil monarch. In the Panjāb, Greek was talked, and Buddhism was the prevailing religion, which was scarcely the case in the south. Barygaza would hardly be the port for a Tamil embassy, with Nelkynda and Muziris at hand. Kadphises had extended his dominions over many "Yavana, Śaka, and Pallava" monarchs, and could appropriately call himself "Mahārāja over 600 kings." Kadphises was familiar with Rome, as is shewn by his imitation of the coins of Augustus. The invitation to Augustus to form an alliance with him, and the offer of a free passage through his domains to Roman citizens, may refer to the overland route through Baktria to China and India. Many curious details about this embassy have been preserved by an eye-witness, Nicolaus of Damascus, who met the party near Antioch. They had started from India about 25 B.C. and had taken four years on the journey. They had suffered much on the road and many had died of fatigue. The length of the journey must have been due to the cumbrous nature of the presents they brought, which included tigers, a partridge as big as an eagle[1], a gigantic python,

[1] This is the *katreus* of Kleitarchus, the monal pheasant from the Himālayas.

huge tortoises, and an armless boy who could shoot arrows and throw darts with his feet! With these ponderous gifts they had been forced to take the overland route, and had evidently experienced great difficulties in convoying them over the passes and through the deserts. Had they gone by sea, the journey would have been over in less than a year. This strange troupe found Augustus in Samos in 21 B.C. The tigers were shewn at the opening of the theatre of Marcellus. Other Indian embassies visited Rome from time to time. We have already referred to one from Ceylon to the Emperor Claudius. Another came to Trajan in 99 A.D. from Kadphises II or Kanishka[1], when the conquest of Mesopotamia had brought the Indian and Roman frontiers within six hundred miles of one another.

In the reign of Claudius, an epoch-making discovery changed the whole aspect of the sea-borne trade between India and Rome. This was the discovery, about 45 A.D. of the existence of the monsoon-winds, blowing regularly across the Indian Ocean, by a captain of the name of Hippalus. The existence of such regular "Etesian" winds had been vaguely known before, and Megasthenes and others had observed that the regular double rainfall of India was due to them. To the Arab sailors, too, the phenomenon

[1] I say this with all reservation. Fleet dates Kanishka at 58 B.C.

was no secret, as the term monsoon, from the Arabic *mauzim*, implies. Hitherto, however, such few Greek vessels as dared to make the voyage from the Red Sea to India had been forced to creep along the Arabian shore and then down the coast of Karmania—an infinitely tedious proceeding. To be becalmed, without compass or map, in the middle of the Indian Ocean was too great a risk to run. Hippalus, however, observing the steady south-west current of the summer months, and learning the secret, perhaps, from an Arab seaman, ventured upon the direct voyage. At first Hippalus merely made the run from Cape Syagrus to Pātala, a distance of 1335 miles, for which he would have the wind directly behind him the whole way. This was subsequently improved upon. It was found that by sailing closer to the wind (the author of the *Periplus* uses the term τραχηλίζοντες, "throwing the ship's head off the wind," evidently a slang word among Alexandrian sailors), it was possible to make Sigerus or Melizigara on the Bombay coast. Later merchants made the voyage shorter still. Striking due east from the port of Cana or from Cape Gardafui, it was found possible to make straight for Damirike, or Malabar, the important pepper-country. For particulars of the voyage we are chiefly indebted to Pliny[1]. After describing the discovery of Hippalus, and the journey

[1] *N.H.* VI. 26; also *Periplus*, § 56.

from Koptos to the sea, he tells that passengers for India usually embarked (at Berenike or Myos Hormos) about midsummer. The voyage to Okēlis, at the mouth of the Red Sea, the favourite port for travellers to India, took just a month. Then, if the Hippalus (the name given to the south-west monsoon, after its discoverer) were blowing, they reached Muziris (Cranganore on the Malabar coast), in forty days. No doubt the time was often bettered in practice, as the distance was only about 2000 miles and a Greek vessel with a good wind could do eighty miles a day[1]. In any case, Alexandria was now brought within a little over two months of the Indian coast. When we remember the thirty months taken by the pioneer of Greek voyages from India to Suez, Skylax of Karyanda, we begin to appreciate the improvements effected in navigation by the first century A.D. Pliny tells us that passengers preferred to embark at Barake[2] in the Pāṇḍya country, rather than at Muziris, on account of the pirates who infested the latter port. To keep off these pirates, East Indiamen had to carry troops of archers. This coast has always

[1] For figures, see Hirth, *China and the Roman Orient*, p. 167 (Shanghai, 1885). Hirth, however, forgets that the revenue-ship belonging to Annius Plocamus, caught in the monsoon off the Arabian coast was blown to the Ceylon coast in *fifteen* days! This, I think, constituted a record for the ancient world. Pliny, *N.H.* VI. 22.

[2] On the outer edge of the great Cochin lagoon. Inside this lagoon was the great port of Nelkynda. *Vide infra.*

been pirate-haunted, to the days of Angria and his Marathas, who gave the English so much trouble. Ptolemy speaks of it as Ariake of the pirates[1]. Barake was the port for the pepper trade, Kottonara (*Kolatta-nadu*, *i.e.* Tellicherry), the centre of the pepper-district. Those returning to Europe had to sail in December, if they wished to take advantage of the north-east monsoon[2]. They could then take advantage of the south and south-west wind in the Red Sea.

We may now turn to the detailed account given in the *Periplus* of the coasting voyage to India, as far as the writer's personal experience went. Coming down the Red Sea, the first port trading direct with India was Muza, the modern Mocha, which sent its ships straight to Barygaza. Evidently these Arabs were rivals of the Greeks, and preferred to use their own vessels. We then come to Okelis, a roadstead with good water and anchorage. Aden (Arabia Felix) the great emporium (which, in the time of the Ptolemies, when the direct voyage to India was not made, had been almost as busy a port of exchange as Alexandria), had lately been sacked by its trade-rivals, and was now in ruins. The writer attributes its overthrow to "Caesar," but as Roman arms never penetrated to Aden, it is supposed that we have here a misreading

[1] Ἀνδρῶν Πειρατῶν. But this has been explained as *Āndhrabhṛitya* (*Bombay Gazetteer, Thāna*, II. 415, note).

[2] Pliny *says* Volturnus, but this must be a slip.

for Eleazar[1] (King of the Frankincense Country) or Charibael[2].

Outside the straits, the first port is Kane, where ships took in water and provisions for their long run. From here the course differed. Vessels for South India struck straight out to sea, past Sokotra or Dioscorida (*Sukhādhāra-dvīpa*, the Isle of the Blest[3]); the rest sailed up the coast of the frankincense country, dark and lowering, with clouds hanging low over the hills. It was desperately unhealthy, and the frankincense was mostly collected by convicts. But its wealth was prodigious. Presently Cape Syagrus (Ras Fārtak) hove in sight, with its headland and fort, and then came the roadstead of Moscha, a port of call for India and a port for the frankincense trade. After this there were no important ports till the traveller came to the Persian Gulf, on which was the port of Ommana. At the mouth of the Euphrates was Apologus, an important harbour, of which, however, our author merely remarks that it imported timber from Barygaza—sandalwood, teak, ebony, and

[1] Eleazer, *Ili azzu*, king of the Λιβανωτοφόροι, 20–65 A.D. Vincent thinks that a Roman expedition from Egypt, or Annius Plocamus on his way to Ceylon in the reign of Claudius (Pliny, *N.H.* VI. 24) sacked Aden. But the *Periplus always* reads Αὐτοκράτωρ, *never* Καῖσαρ, for the Roman Emperor (*e.g.* § 23). Hence the reading *must* be corrupt.

[2] Charibael, *Kariba-Il*, Blessed by God, king of the Homerites and Sabaites, 40–70 A.D.

[3] Hence Agatharchides, § 103, translates it as νῆσοι εὐδαίμονες.

blackwood. The importation of Indian wood was as old as the days of Sennacherib, and it is found in ancient Chaldean and Assyrian temples.

We now come to the most interesting part of the narrative—our author's notes on the Indian ports which he visited. The first of these is the harbour called by the Greeks Barbarikon, whatever the Indian name may have been[1]. It was on the middle mouth of the Indus, and the cargoes were disembarked here and sent in boats to Minnagara, the capital of Sind. This was probably Pātala. It was called *Min-nagara* (City of the Min or Śaka), as Sind was then in the possession of "Parthian Princes who were always driving one another out." These were, no doubt, the Indo-Parthians, who had been turned out of the Panjāb by the Kushāns. When our author found them, the dynasty had evidently already relapsed into anarchy. The writer correctly notes that the natives called the Indus *Sinthus* (*Sindhu*)[2]. The exports of Sind (which had not yet been eclipsed by the southern ports), were costus (Skt. *kushṭha, Saussurea lappa*) an aromatic plant from Kashmīr used for perfumes; lycium or berberry, a cosmetic fashionable in Rome; nard (citronella), gems, indigo, skins, and lastly silk from China. Silk was destined

[1] The Greeks always corrupted an Indian word to its nearest Greek equivalent. Perhaps in this case it was something like Bahārdipur (Schoff, *ad loc.*); see p. 119, note.

[2] § 40.

to become an immensely important article of commerce. The expeditions of the Baktrian monarchs, Demetrius and Menander[1], and of the Kushān kings, had opened out the great trade route which runs from Balkh to the historic "Stone Tower" of Sarikol. Some of the silk also found its way through Nepal to the Ganges and thence to the Malabar coast[2]. Later on, it was taken straight from China to Rome, by the land-route from Sarikol to Balkh, Hekatompylus, Ekbatana, Ktesiphon, Hira, and Charax, and then by sea to Petra, Tyre, and the Levant[3]. Ptolemy tells us of the Macedonian merchant named Maes or Titianus, whose caravans went through the wild Bolor mountains to the Stone Tower, a frontier fort on a desolate crag. Here the Chinese, whose capital was "a seven months' journey away," met them with the silk[4]. Silk was the rage in Rome, and this extravagant habit is the occasion of one of Pliny's homilies[5]. For a long time the origin of silk was a mystery to the Romans. The yarn was woven at places like Cos. It was popularly supposed to grow on trees, a belief which perhaps arose from travellers' tales of the cocoons of the silkworms being

[1] Strabo, XI. II. I. [2] *Periplus*, § 64.

[3] Hirth, *China and the Roman Orient* (Shanghai, 1885), *passim*.

[4] *Geog*. I. 12. 8. The road went through the land of the *Kasii*. Is this Kashgar?

[5] *N.H.* XXI. 8.

attached to the mulberry leaves on which they feed. Hence Vergil's

> Velleraque ut foliis depectant tenvia Seres[1].

Aristotle, however, knew a great deal more than this about the matter, though his account was evidently disbelieved[2]. The Chinese jealously guarded their secret till the days of Justinian, when two adventurous monks smuggled silkworms' eggs to Constantinople in a hollow cane.

Passing the treacherous Ran of Kacch, our traveller next put in at the ancient harbour of Barygaza (perhaps *Bhṛighu-Kaccha*), the most famous of the Indian ports trading with the West, until it was eclipsed, after 47 A.D., by its southern rivals. It is the modern Broach. It lay on the river Narmadā, and was difficult of access on account of shoals, and the extraordinary ebb and flow of the tide. At one moment the tide would flow right out, leaving vessels stranded; at the next, it returned with a roar "like an advancing army," and woe to the luckless vessel caught unprepared[3]. These intimate touches make us feel that the *Periplus* is a narrative of actual experiences. At Broach the writer found the coins of Menander and Apollodotus still in circulation. Specie was also imported, native Indian coinage being, as usual, scarce and bad. Our author was no scholar, and he gravely accepted the story that the remains of great shrines, forts,

[1] *Georg.* II. 121. [2] *Hist. An.* V. 19. 11. [3] § 45.

and wells in the Broach district were relics of Alexander's invasion. He also says that Alexander "penetrated to the Ganges[1]." The fertile coast-country between Broach and the Indus, the writer calls Syrastrene, obviously *Surāshṭra*, the name still surviving in Surat. The trade, export and import, of the district, was immense[2]. The exports included the various Indian condiments and spices, muslins, and stones: the imports, specie, unguents, singing boys, and "choice girls for the Royal harem." These, doubtless, were the *Yavanīs* of the king's bodyguard, already referred to. The capital of the district was a second "Minnagara," or Śaka city, probably Madhyamikā, but which of the numerous Śaka dynasties was reigning there at the time, it is impossible to say. The old capital had been the historic city of Oẓene or Ujjain, the chief town of Mālwā, and the seat of the Viceroy of Western India in the days of the Mauryas. It was now temporarily abandoned. A few years later, it became again the capital under the Śaka satrap Chastana, the Tiasṭanes of Ptolemy. Ships from the Red Sea began to arrive about July, as soon as the south-west monsoon had set in, and they were met by Government pilot-boats, and moored in regular basins, where the bore of the Narmadā was least dangerous. In this statement we have

[1] Is the true reading *Menander* for Alexander in these two passages?

[2] A detailed list is given in §§ 48–50.

a further piece of evidence of the advanced state of Indian shipping[1]. The monarch reigning in Gujarat (Ariake) was *Mambarus*, who may be Nahapāna[2], the Kshaharāta chieftain who succeeded Bhūmaka[3]. Nahapāna was afterwards conquered by the Āndhra monarch Vilivāyakura II[4]. His head-quarters may have been at Nāsik, close to which town a large hoard of his coins has recently come to light. They bear an inscription in barbarous Greek characters, and a head obviously imitated from Baktrian or Roman types. Evidently Nahapāna's trade brought him in considerable wealth, and brought him into contact with Graeco-Roman influence.

Our traveller now[5] goes on to describe the Deccan, the seat of the great Āndhra kingdom. Deccan (*Dakkhinābada*[6]) he correctly derives from δάχανος, south. Beyond the Ghauts, the land is wild and desolate, full of tigers, apes, and huge pythons[7]. The principal ports were Ter

[1] Regulations for harbour-masters and pilots are laid down in the *Kauṭilīya Artha Śāstra*. See App. to Ch. III.

[2] Wilson in *J.R.A.S. Bengal*, June, 1904.

[3] Rapson in *J.R.A.S.* 1904, p. 371.

[4] V. Smith dates this at 126 A.D. but this is inconsistent with the accepted date of the *Periplus*.

[5] § 52.

[6] Skt. *Dakshiṇāpatha*. Δαχιναβάδης καλεῖται ἡ χώρα· δάχανος γὰρ καλεῖται ὁ νότος τῇ αὐτῶν γλώσσῃ. Here we have another personal touch.

[7] This agrees with what Hiuen Tsiang and other travellers tell us, and was still true of the Deccan till quite recent times.

(Tāgara), Sopāra, Paithān and Kalyān, these being supplied with goods from the central part of India by the great high road running through Daulatabad to Hyderabad. Kalyān and Sopāra, the chief harbours in the days of "the elder Saraganus" (probably *Arishṭa Śātakarṇi*), had, since the accession of the weak king Sandanes (*Sundara Śātakarṇi*), been blockaded by the men-of-war from the rival port of Broach, who towed vessels off to their own harbour and made them unload there! Here we have another interesting side-light on contemporary Indian history.

The remaining ports of the Deccan were:

(i) Mandagora, probably Bankot.
(ii) Palaipatmai, probably Dhābol or Pāripatana.
(iii) Melizigara, probably Jaigaḍ.
(iv) Byzantium, probably Vizādrog[1].
(v) Togarum, probably Devgaḍ.
(vi) Auranoboas or Tyrannoboas, probably Aranyavāha or Mālvan.

Also the following islands:

(i) Sesikrienae, probably Vengurla.
(ii) Aegidii, probably Angidīva or Goa.
(iii) Kaenitae, probably Kārwāḍ.

[1] This was *not* a Byzantine colony! The Greeks always transliterated a Hindu name so as to be as like as possible to some well-known Greek word. We do the same, *e.g.* *Hobson-Jobson* and many other ludicrous instances. The *Apollo* Bunder at Bombay is the *Pālvā Bandar*, for instance.

After this, the traveller arrived at the Tamil country, Damirike[1]. The chief ports mentioned are Muziris, in the country of Kerobothra or Keralaputra, the Western Tamil kingdom, and Nelkynda, in the kingdom of Pāṇḍya (Pandion) or Madurā. Muziris, as we have already seen, was shunned by travellers on account of bad anchorage and the pirates. It is almost certainly *Muyiri-kotta*, the modern Cranganore[2]. Nelkynda (*Nil-kantha*, perhaps) was somewhere in the Cochin backwaters. At the mouth of the backwaters stood Barake, the port mentioned by Pliny. Nelkynda became about this time the most important of the Indian ports. This was partly due to the blockade of the Northern Deccan coast by the ships of Broach. The chief reason, however, is to be sought in the pepper-trade, for which, after the epoch-making discovery of Hippalus, it became the chief port. After this, it completely eclipsed even Broach[3]. The exports of Nelkynda were most multifarious. Pepper and other condiments, drugs like spikenard and malobathrum, jewels like beryls, pearls, diamonds and sapphires, ivory and silk from Bengal, and tortoise-shell from the Golden Chersonese, were the chief. As we have already noticed, the

[1] This is surely the correct reading. MSS. *Limirike*, which is meaningless.

[2] Not Mangalore, as formerly held.

[3] It is mentioned by Pliny, Ptolemy, the author of the *Geography of Ravenna*, and in the Peutinger Tables.

enormous extent of the trade with Southern India in the first century A.D. is evidenced by the great numbers of Roman coins found there. There seems little doubt that eventually regular colonies of Roman traders sprang up in the Madras Presidency. The Peutinger Tables represent a temple of Augustus at Muziris. There was a "Yavana" colony at the mouth of the Kāviri river. Ptolemy tells of meeting people who had resided in the Madurā district "for a long time[1]," and the great numbers of copper coins of little value found there point in the same direction. Roman soldiers, like the Vikings and the Swiss in later days, enlisted in the service of foreign kings, and "dumb Mlecchas," or "powerful Yavanas" in complete armour attending native princes are often mentioned in Tamil literature[2]. Further than Nelkynda, our traveller evidently did not go. Like the great majority of Indian merchants of his time, he made the coasting voyage up the Arabian shores, to the head of the Persian Gulf, along the Mekrān to the mouth of the Indus, and then down the Indian coast to Cochin. His account is a reminiscence of personal experiences on this run. At

[1] ἐντεῦθεν εἰσπλευσάντων καὶ χρόνον πλεῖστον ἐπελθόντων. *Geog.* Prol. I. 17.

[2] Mukerji, *Indian Shipping*, p. 128 ff. collects the evidence for this. See also Sewell, *Roman Coins found in India* (*J.R.A.S.* 1904, p. 391). Pillay, *The Tamils eighteen hundred years ago*, Ch. III; Vincent Smith, *Early History of India* (1907), p. 400.

Nelkynda, no doubt, he discharged his cargoes, loaded his holds with pepper, cinnamon, silks, muslins, and perhaps with a box or two of pearls, sapphires, and tortoise-shell, and waiting for the north-east winds of December, spread his sails for the long voyage back to the mouth of the Red Sea. But before he left Nelkynda, he gathered, no doubt from other sea-captains at anchor within the backwaters, many valuable facts about the east coast of India as far as the mouth of the Ganges, and these he has briefly recorded. Proceeding on his voyage, the traveller comes to cape Kumāri, where dwells a goddess (*Kumārī* or Devī), and where, we are told, is a shrine and monastery, where men and women dedicate themselves to a life of chastity in her honour, and perform ablutions. This is still true of the pilgrims who visit this holy spot. After this comes the Coast Land, the *Chola Maṇḍalam* or Chola-coast, the modern Coromandel. Its ports were Kamara, the *Khaberis emporium* of Ptolemy, at the mouth of the Kaveri; Poduca, *i.e.* Puducheri or Pondicherry; and Soptama—*Su-patana*, the "fair city" of Madras. Here there was a flourishing trade in pearls and muslins, and ships from Bengal frequently put in. Travellers, were struck by the *sangāra*[1], or catamarans, large vessels made of logs, and the sea-going *kolandia*. To the Coromandel coast, says our author, went a very large proportion of the exports from Rome.

[1] Caldwell says this is the Malayalam *jangāla*.

Of the neighbouring island of Ceylon he knows very little, but like all the writers of his time, he thinks it a vast island projecting far into the ocean. Then comes Masalia, the Masulipatam district, with a great trade in muslins, and Dosarene, the *Darśana* or holy land of Orissa, with its trade in ivory. After this, our writer becomes very vague. Further on lies the Ganges, with a port at its mouth (probably Tāmralipti) whence come the Benares muslins, Chinese silk, and malobathrum. A most interesting description of the Mongolian hillmen who collect the malobathrum on the Chinese border concludes the *Periplus*. "Every year, on the borders of This (China), assembles a tribe of men with stunted bodies and broad, flat faces. They are timid and peaceful, and almost wild. They are called *Besatae* (*vishāda*, dullness, stupidity [1]). They come with their families bearing baskets of what appear to be thin grape-leaves. They meet in a place halfway between their own land and China, and hold a fair, spreading out the baskets and using them as mats. After this they return to their own land. Then the natives who are on the watch take these mats and pick out the leaves, which they call 'petri' (*patra*, leaves). They then press them into layers and fasten them with fibres taken from the mats. These they make into balls of three sizes whence come the three grades of malobathrum to be had

[1] So Lassen, *Ind. Alt.* III. 8, but Lassen's imaginary adjective *vaishada*, dull, does not exist. See p. 147.

in India." Here we have a description of the "silent barter" carried on by many shy, wild tribes all over the world, and still practised by the Veddas of Ceylon. The goods to be bought are left in a clearing, and the purchaser takes them, replacing them by their equivalent in value. Pliny says Sinhalese merchants went to this mart[1], and Kosmas Indikopleustes saw a similar system employed in Ethiopia.

APPENDIX

SOME NOTES ON INDIAN DRUGS AND PERFUMES

Indian drugs and perfumes were known indirectly in Europe at a very early date. The first extensive account of them is given in Theophrastus' *History of Plants*. But Pliny's account is much fuller, and there are many valuable remarks on this important trade in the *Periplus*. The following notes deal with some of the principal plants.

Costus. Skt. *kushṭha*, modern *kut-lākḍī*, called also *uplet* in Karachi, and *puchuk* in the Far East. It is the root of the *Saussurea lappa* (hence the Roman name *Radix*), and grows in the Himālayas. It was exported from Barygaza and Barbarikon, and fetched five denarii a pound in Rome, where it was used for making perfumes and for cooking. It is still exported from Kashmīr (where it is a state monopoly), *via* Karachi and Bombay, to China and Japan, where it is apparently used as incense. About 2000 cwt., valued at about Rs 40,000, are exported annually. Hamilton (*New*

[1] *N.H.* VI. 22, 24. Kennedy denies this and reads *Cheras* for *Seres*, *J.R.A.S.* 1904, p. 359. Other references to the silent trade are Herod. IV. 196 (Libya); Ammianus Marcellinus, XXIII. 6. 68 (Seres); Pomponius Mela, III. 8. 60 (Himālayan tribes).

Account, I. 128), writing about 1720, says, "There are great quantities exported from Surat and thence to China, where it bears a good price. For being all idolaters and burning incense before their images, this root beaten into fine powder ...will burn a long time like a match, sending forth a fine smoke whose smell is very grateful."

Lycium. Exported from Barygaza and Barbarikon, was the bark and fruit of several species of Himālayan berberry, used for preparing an astringent medicine, and for a cosmetic (Pliny, XXIV. 72).

Malabathrum, Cassia. Both these were the products of the cinnamon tree, a kind of laurel, several varieties of which were used in ancient trade. The true home of the cinnamon plant was, of course, the cinnamon country of the Somali coast, and the adjacent parts of Arabia Felix. Pure cinnamon fetched 1500 denarii per pound. This was the stems and bark of the tree, and was used for making unguents, for incense, and for a condiment. Malabathrum, on the other hand, consisted of the *leaves* of a cinnamon plant (perhaps *C. tamala*), used for the manufacture of a famous unguent, known chiefly from the reference in Horace (II. 7. 89), and came from the Himālayas.

Curiously enough, Ceylon cinnamon, so famous in Dutch days, was not known to the ancients. It is impossible, in this limited space to give details of the cinnamon trade, which has continued from Egyptian and Jewish times down to the present day.

Frankincense. True frankincense, the product of five species of the genus *Boswellia*, comes from the Hadhramaut country, and is imported to India and China, the port of export being Dafār (sometimes supposed to be the Sapphara Metropolis of Ptolemy). Its Arabian origin is indicated by its name *olibanum* (al-luban). There are, however, several gums used in India instead of incense. Among these, *bdellium* (Pliny, XII. 19) was one of the commonest. It is a gum resembling myrrh, and the product of several species of the *Balsamodendron*. It grows chiefly on the slopes of the Hindu

Kush, and was exported from Barbarikon and Barygaza. It was worth three denarii a pound. *Storax*, or Benzoin, the gum of trees of the genus *Styracaceae*, is the modern Indian *ud* or incense. It was apparently not common in India, being one of the imports mentioned in the *Periplus*. *Myrrh* was the gum of another tree of the genus *Balsamodendron*. Its Sanskrit name is *vola*, whence the modern Indian *bol*. Pliny, XII. 35, gives a long account of the collection of the gum (*stactē*). The best sort fetched 40 denarii per pound. Some of the Acacias produce fragrant gums, used for the adulteration of incense, and employed for similar purposes.

Spikenard. This was the stem and leaves of the *Nardostachys Jatamansi*, a plant of the Valerian class found in the Himālayas. It was used for making the famous "ointment of spikenard" which is chiefly known to English readers from the episode in St Mark XIV. 3. It fetched from 40 to 75 denarii a pound. It was exported from Barygaza, from the Malabar coast (whence it arrived from the mouth of the Ganges), and from Bengal. It must not be confused with *nard*, which was apparently an essential oil extracted from the citronella or ginger-grass, found in Baluchistān and exported from Barbarikon. See Pliny, XII. 26 ff.

(For further details, see Watt's *Commercial Products of India*, articles under the various headings in the *Encyclopedia Britannica*, the numerous scattered notes of great value in Yule's *Marco Polo* (3rd edition, Murray, 1903), and in the *Gazetteer of the Bombay Presidency*. See also Sir George Birdwood's articles in the *Transactions of the Linnaean Society*, vols. XXVII–XXVIII, and *Journal of the Royal Society of Arts*, June 1914, Gustav Oppert's *Trade with Ancient India*, Madras, 1879, and U. C. Dutt's *Materia Medica of the Hindus*, revised by K. A. Sen, Calcutta 1901.)

CHAPTER VII

INDIA AND THE ROMAN EMPIRE (CONTINUED)

TRADE between India and Rome continued to thrive steadily during the second and third centuries A.D. There was a temporary lull in the demand for luxuries after the extraordinary outburst of extravagance which culminated in the reign of Nero, but this did not have a very serious effect upon commerce. Roman Emperors took an increasing interest in Eastern questions, and, as we may see from the writers of the time, the bounds of geographical knowledge were slowly but surely extended. Trajan[1] during his Parthian expedition, travelled to the mouth of the Euphrates and watched the ships spreading their sails for India. He is said to have dreamed of making an expedition to the country himself. He pushed the Roman frontier to within six hundred miles of Indian territory. He entertained an Indian embassy regally, giving its members senators' seats at the theatre[2]. In the reign of Marcus

[1] Dion Cassius, LXVII. 28.

[2] *Ibid.* IX. 58.

Aurelius, Avidius Cassius fought another successful campaign against Parthia and took the winter capital of Ktesiphon.

In spite of temporary set-backs caused by these wars, the land-borne trade between Europe and the East flourished exceedingly. We have already mentioned that it consisted chiefly of Chinese silk, but Indian goods found their way, wholly or partly, by these routes to Europe in considerable quantities as well[1]. Great cities sprang up, created by this traffic. One of the chief roads—the one which ran from the Parthian capital at Hekatompylus—passed through Ekbatana and Ktesiphon. At Ktesiphon it branched off in several directions, the main track running through Mesopotamia, crossing the Tigris by the famous flying bridge between Zeugma and Apamea, and ending at the port of Antioch[2]. Another important branch of the road ran to Palmyra, and then to Damascus, Gaza, Tyre, and Sidon, and joined the network of highways which converged at Petra[3]. The great city of

[1] The chief passages referring to the overland route are: Pliny, *N.H.* VI. 17; Strabo, XI. 7. 3; *ibid.* XII. 2. 17; *ibid.* XIV. 2. 29; *ibid.* XVI. 2. 3 and the Σταθμοὶ Παρθικοί of Isidore of Charax.

[2] Zeugma transitu Euphratis nobile. Ex adverso Apameam Seleukus, idem utriusque conditor, ponte iunxerat. Pliny, *N.H.* V. 24. See also Bunbury, *Hist. Anc. Geog.* §§ 17–20.

[3] Huc convenit utrumque bivium, eorum qui Syria Palmyram petiere et eorum qui a Gaza venerunt. Pliny, *N.H.* VI. 28. 144.

Petra played a very large part in Eastern trade, more, however, Arabic than Indian. Most of the Indian goods which came up the Red Sea naturally found their way to Alexandria, but some were unshipped at Leuke Kome for Petra [1]. These no doubt included silks and other stuffs which went to Tyre to be re-dyed. Gaza and Rhinokolura (the latter originally an Ethiopian convict settlement), were both convenient ports from Petra for the Mediterranean. Petra was a lovely spot, built in an oasis, with springs and gardens, and a large cosmopolitan population. It was visited by Strabo's friend Athenodorus, and its noble ruins are still an object of admiration. It owed its great prosperity to the caravans from the mouth of the Euphrates, and from the spice, incense, and gold lands of Arabia Felix which converged in its bazaars. It was reduced, however, by Trajan in 105 A.D. for helping the Parthians, when Palmyra took its place as the great *entrepôt* of the Oriental land-trade, till she, too, fell before the Roman arms in 273 A.D. after a career of unexampled splendour and prosperity.

Meanwhile, the sea-borne trade with the far East was also progressing. The Parthian war of 162–165 A.D. and the terrible outbreak of plague at Babylon, had caused something like a panic in the silk traffic, and, a mercantile mission, pretending to come from the Emperor Marcus Aurelius, but really no doubt sent by the rich

[1] Strabo, XVI. 4. 24.

merchants of Antioch or Alexandria, reached the court of the Chinese monarch Huan-ti in October, 166 A.D. They represented to the king that their master had always desired to send embassies to China, but the Parthians had wished to carry on the trade in Chinese silks, and for this reason they had been cut off from direct communication. They therefore represented themselves as having been sent by Antun king of Ta-tsin (Antonius King of Syria), who offered ivory, rhinoceros horns, and tortoise-shell from the frontier of Annam. They brought no jewels, says the Chinese annalist, a fact which makes him suspect their story. However, from that date, he continues, direct intercourse between China and the West by sea began. No doubt the merchandise went from Annam to Nelkynda and was there shipped to Alexandria and Antioch[1].

Ptolemy, the great Alexandrian geographer, writing about this time, chiefly from information collected by Marinus of Tyre, exhibits a much fuller knowledge of the Asiatic coast than his predecessors, from which we may infer that the mission to the Chinese court was only part of a general pushing forward of Roman trade with the Far East. The author of the *Periplus* knew

[1] I follow Hirth, *China and the Roman Orient*, text p. 42, and commentary, pp. 173–8. See also Reinaud, *Relations de l'Empire Romain avec l'Asie Oriental*, p. 184; Priaulx, *Indian Embassies to Rome* (*J.R.A.S.* XIX. 294) and Yule's *Cathay and the Way Thither*.

little or nothing of the coast beyond the mouth of the Ganges. Ptolemy goes a great deal further, though, possibly because he had to depend upon the reports of illiterate seamen, his statements are often very confused and vague. He mixes up Java and Sumatra ; he says nothing of the Straits of Malacca, and he thinks that the Chinese coast, instead of trending northward, bends southward to meet the shores of Africa !

Before we find fault with a system which led to such extraordinary results, we should remember the difficulties with which Ptolemy had to contend. He was dependent for his information upon ignorant sailors, who often misspelt hopelessly the very names of the ports at which they touched. He had only their word for the direction in which they sailed from port to port, and this was often entirely wrong ; and for distance, as he himself confesses, he had to be content with calculating from the average run of a ship per day, with deductions to allow for irregularities of the coast, and other disturbing factors. The result of attempting to plot a map upon such *data* may be seen from the charts of Ptolemy. It led to the strangest contortions of the coast of India itself. Ptolemy seems to be quite unaware of the southward trend of the great peninsula ; he thinks that Barygaza is very little to the north of Cape Kory, while Palura is actually to the south of it ! In fact he pictures the coast of India, and of the country beyond, as running from west to east in a more or less continuous line, only broken by the Gangetic Gulf or Bay of Bengal. From Cape Kory to the Ganges, we have a series of towns, of which the most interesting is perhaps one, not named, which lies between Maesolia and Palura. Maesolia, the Masalia of the *Periplus*, is probably the Masulipatam district, and Palura, at the beginning of the Gangetic Gulf, lies a little further to the north[1]. From this place ships set out on the voyage to the Far East[2]. Crossing the Bay of Bengal, they arrived at Sada in the Silver Country[3], and from Sada to Temala or Tamala near Cape Negrais. From here to a port called Zaba[4], was a voyage of twenty days; and from Zaba about the same distance to Kattigara. On this part of the voyage, however, Ptolemy admits himself to be very doubtful. His information is taken from Marinus, who in turn derived his from a trader named Alexander. Alexander's expression "some days," says Ptolemy, may mean anything,—few or many.

Proceeding up the coast of India from Palura, Ptolemy arrives at the mouth of the Ganges. He is the first Western writer to mention the

[1] Colonel Yule puts it as far north as the Ganjām river.

[2] ἀφετήριον τῶν εἰς Χρυσῆν πλεόντων.

[3] VII. 2. 3. I. 13. 7.

[4] VII. 2. 6. It was at the head of the Gulf of Siam (the Great Gulf). Yule identifies it with Champā, and looks for it on the west coast of Camboja and probably near the Kampot or Kang-Kao river. (*Ind. Ant.* VI. 228.)

great Ganges delta. Even the writer of the *Periplus* says nothing of this, and Strabo and all earlier writers are silent upon the point, if we except Vergil's doubtful reference to the "seven calm streams" of that river[1]. Ptolemy assigns to the Ganges five mouths[2]. From the Ganges he goes on to Trans-Gangetic India[3]. First we arrive at the land of the Airrhadii, *i.e.* Further India from the Ganges to the Tokosanna or Arakan river; then we come to the Silver Country, Arakan and Pegu; then to Besynga or Bassein; and finally to the Golden Chersonese, the Malay Peninsula. The name is a translation of the Sanskrit *Suvarṇabhūmi*, applied to the Irrawady delta, the Burmese documents similarly styling their frontier as the Sonaparānta (Aurea Regio)[4]. After this, we arrive at the Great Cape (Cape Camboja) and the Great Gulf or Gulf of Siam. At the western end of this gulf lay Zabæ or Zaba, the port already mentioned for travellers sailing for Kattigara[5].

The inhabitants of Burma-Siam are described as being "fair, shaggy, squat-figured and flat-nosed,"—a very good description on the whole. It is clear, from the frequent mention of marts, river-mouths and the like, that Ptolemy gets his information from traders who have been up

[1] *Aen.* IX. 30–31. [2] VII. 1. 18. [3] VII. 2. 2.

[4] Suvarṇabhūmi, as we have already seen (Ch. II), was known to merchants in the *Jātaka* days.

[5] VII. 2. 6.

and down the coast. Even more interesting is the evidence that these traders penetrated beyond the Sunda Straits into the Eastern Seas. Ptolemy had a good deal to say about the Malay Archipelago. Among the "Islands of Transgangetic India," he mentions Sindae, inhabited by cannibals; the Isle of Good Luck (Ἀγαθοῦ δαίμονος); the Sabadeibae and Barusae Isles, also inhabited by cannibals; the island of Iabadius, or Isle of Barley, very fertile, producing much gold and having as its capital Argyre, or Silver Town, at its western extremity; the Isle of the Satyrs, where the inhabitants have tails; and the magnetic rocks of the Maniolae, which attract ships, unless they are built with wooden pegs instead of nails. Of these islands, Sindae[1], the Isle of Good Luck, and the Sabadeibae Isles, have been located off the coast of Sumatra; the Barusae Islands are probably the Nicobars; while the Isle of Satyrs no doubt took its name from the apes which the mariners saw on it. The story of the fabulous rocks of Maniolae, which attracted ships, is familiar to readers of the *Arabian Nights*. Far more important, however, is the reference to the island of Iabadius, or *Java dvīpa*. The mention of this important island shews a very great advance in Western knowledge of the Far East. That there is no doubt about the

[1] Lassen, *Ind. Alt.* III. 250, sees in this name a reference to Indian traders (*Sindhu*). Yule thinks that the name survives in Sundar Fulât. Sabadeibae is *Saba-dvīpa*.

identification, is shewn by the fact that Ptolemy knows that the word signifies in Sanskrit the "Isle of Barley[1]." It is characteristic, however, of the vague and inaccurate information supplied by his illiterate informers, that Ptolemy confuses Java with the neighbouring island of Sumatra. The description given is obviously of Sumatra and not of Java at all. Sumatra, not Java, is rich in gold, and Argyre, the capital on the western extremity of the island, is in all probability Achin[2]. Java became later an important Hindu colony, as its great ruins testify; both it and Cambodia became the seats of important bodies of settlers, perhaps partly owing to the extension of the China trade. Java, if we may judge from the narrative of Fa Hian, was an *entrepôt* for traffic with the Far East, like the Arabian ports in the West; and the island was visited again by Ibn Batuta in the fourteenth century. After rounding the coast of Indo-China, Ptolemy's account becomes more and more vague. He thinks that the coast-line, instead of bearing away to the north, turns southwards, finally connecting Asia and Africa, and enclosing the Indian Ocean so as to form, like the Mediterranean Sea, a huge landlocked expanse of water. After crossing the Gulf of Beasts (the Gulf of Tongking), we come to Kattigara, the last port in the known expanse of the ancient world, and here Ptolemy's

1 Sanskrit *yava*, 'barley.'

2 Bunbury, II. 643; Yule, *Marco Polo*, II. 266, note.

account ends. Kattigara is probably Kian-chi in Tongking, for we learn from the Chinese annalist who tells us of the Roman embassy to China that the Romans (Ta-tsin) came there in great numbers to trade. Inland lay the great "Metropolis of China[1]," which had *not*, says Ptolemy, the brazen walls or other fabulous attributes usually assigned to it. It was probably Nankin. It had already been vaguely known to the Western world as a vast city exporting silk to Barygaza and the Ganges[2].

This concludes Ptolemy's account of the geography of India. He is, unfortunately, of little use for our purpose, for his great work is mathematical, not descriptive, and throws little or no light upon the condition of India in his day. "His object," says McCrindle, "in composing it, was not, like that of the ordinary geographer, to describe places, but to correct and reform the map of the world in accordance with the increased knowledge which had been acquired of distant countries and with the improved state of science. He therefore limits his treatise to an exposition of the geometrical principles on which geography should be based and to a determination of the position of places on the

[1] The Sinae were the people of south-eastern China, known chiefly by trade from the sea and with Eastern India. The Seres or Silk-people lay to the west and north of the Sinae, and came in contact with the west by trade over the Pamirs.

[2] Ptolemy, *Geog.* VII. 3. 6; *Periplus*, § 64.

surface of the earth by their latitude and longitude." "It differs from Strabo's production," he adds, "as the skeleton does from the living body."

With Ptolemy we come to an end of the series of eminent geographers who have treated in detail the subject of India. The last Greek writer to deal with the subject of Indian travel is the monk Kosmas Indikopleustes, nearly five centuries later, who wrote when the mists of the Middle Ages were fast settling down upon the ancient world. The gap is, however, filled in, in a most interesting fashion, by a series of incidental notices appearing in philosophical and religious writers, Christian and pagan, of the time, who often exhibit an unexpectedly intimate knowledge of Indian philosophy, religion, and social observances. It is instructive, moreover, to observe the steady growth of knowledge about India which these writers exhibit, and to contrast them with Strabo, who knows little more than what he has learnt from Megasthenes, over two centuries before him. This intimacy was probably due both to the frequency with which Alexandrian and Syrian traders visited India, and also to the presence of Indians in Alexandria[1].

As we have already seen, there were probably

[1] The first Alexandrian to visit India was Skythianus a contemporary of the Apostles (*J.R.A.S.* xx. 267). Ptolemy and Dion Cassius mention Indians in Alexandria (*As. Res.* III. 53). So does St Chrysostom, *Or.* XXXII. 373. The first Indian mention of Alexandria is in the *Gārgī Saṃhitā* (*Yavanapura*).

Roman colonies in Southern India, whose inhabitants, settling in the country for a considerable time, acquired a greater intimacy with Indian customs than had been possible before. The Manicheans owed many of their curious tenets to the Indian lore acquired in his Eastern travels by Terebinthus[1], and the Gnostic heresy shews similar traces of Eastern influence. The debt of Neo-platonism to Oriental sources is indisputable, and when we observe the extent of the knowledge about Eastern beliefs exhibited, not only by Origen, but by orthodox writers like Clement and St Jerome, we cannot help wondering whether Christianity does not owe some of its developments,—monasticism and relic-worship, for instance,—to Buddhist influence. But this subject will be dealt with in a subsequent chapter.

It should be remembered that from this time to the days of the great migration to Java, Indian shipping itself developed considerably. Mention has been already made of the ships, of considerable size, employed from the earliest times by Indian merchants. It was in the days of Eudoxus that the first Indian, a shipwrecked sailor, rescued by chance from a watery grave, reached Alexandria. The subsequent expansion in trade is marked by the rules for merchandise, shipping, and port-dues found in the Code of Manu[2]. It was probably

[1] One tradition says to Skythianus, the Alexandrian mentioned above. Terebinthus was his disciple.

[2] III. 158 ff.

some time in the first century A.D. that the first or Eastern invasion of Java, by colonists from Kalinga, took place. Subsequent invasions by large bodies of adventurers from Gujarat and the Western ports, are probably some three or four centuries later[1]. The interesting treatise on shipping, the *Yuktikalpataru* of Bhoja Narapati, may belong to this period. In this pamphlet, detailed directions for shipbuilding are given, and ships 176 cubits long, fitted with cabins, are referred to[2].

One of the most curious relics of the trade between Egypt and India was unearthed recently at Oxyrhynchus[3]. It is a papyrus of a Greek farce of the second century A.D. and contains the story of a Greek lady named Charition who has been shipwrecked on the Kanarese coast. The locality is identified by the fact that the king of the country addresses his retinue as Ἰνδῶν πρόμοι, and also by the discovery of the learned Dr Hultzsch[4], that the barbarous jargon in which they address one another is actually

[1] The first Hindu colony reached Java from Kalinga about 75 A.D. The first king was Āditya. The earliest inscriptions are in Vengi (*i.e.* Kalinga) dialect, and *Kling* is the Javanese for India. The immigrants from Gujarat were Buddhists.

[2] Mukerji, *Indian Shipping*, Ch. I. Rajendralāl Mitra, *Not. Skt. MSS.* I. 271.

[3] *Oxyrhynchus Papyri*, Grenfell and Hunt, 1903, No. 413, p. 41 ff.

[4] *Hermes*, XXXIX. p. 307. In the same way a Carthaginian in the *Mercator* of Plautus speaks Punic.

Kanarese! The identification of the dialect is made possible by one of the characters, who interprets some of the words into Greek[1].

Of other writers who refer to India, the earliest is Dio Chrysostom, who lived in the reign of Trajan and died in or after 117 A.D.[2] He mentions Indians among the cosmopolitan crowds to be found in the bazaars of Alexandria, and he says that they came "by way of trade." They made various assertions about their country, he adds, but they were not men of a very reputable class[3]. Chrysostom's information about India, however, is not very accurate or striking. He makes the misleading statement that the poetry of Homer, the woes of Andromache and Priam, and the death of Hector and Achilles, had been translated into the Indian language and modes of expression[4]. Chrysostom has led many people to imagine that Greek dramas were actually performed and understood in India, but this can never have been the case. Probably he was led astray by the accidental resemblances between certain Indian and Greek stories. The plot of the *Iliad*,—the rape of Helen,—for instance, bears a distant

[1] Thus he interprets κόττως as πιεῖν δός. The Kanarese for this is *koḍisu*. And so forth.

[2] For the literature of the subject, see especially Priaulx, *Indian Travellers*, *Life of Apollonius of Tyana*, and *Indian Embassies to Rome* (*J.R.A.S.* XIX. p. 294).

[3] *Or.* XXXII. 373, ed. Morell.

[4] *Or.* LIII. 544, ed. Morell.

likeness to the rape of Sītā in the *Rāmāyaṇa.* His assertion is repeated by Aelian[1].

Much more accurate is the knowledge possessed by the Christian writer Clement of Alexandria, who died about 220 A.D. Clement derived much of his information from his tutor Pantaenus, one of the earliest Christian missionaries to visit India[2]. Clement starts by telling us that the Brahmin sect take no wine and abstain from flesh. The latter was a doctrine which found much favour with Neo-platonists (as we see from Porphyry's Περὶ ἀποχῆς τῶν ἐμψύχων). He goes on to add that they worship Pan and Herakles,—probably Brahmā, the "All-God," and Śiva,—and abstain from women. But the most important of his statements are that the Brahmins despise death and set no value on life, *because they believe in transmigration* (παλιγγενεσία); and that the Σεμνοί (*Śramaṇa* or Buddhists) *worship a kind of pyramid beneath which they imagine that the bones of a divinity of some kind lie buried*[3]. This remarkable allusion to the Buddhist *stūpa* is the earliest reference in Western literature to a unique feature of Buddhism, and must have been derived from some informant intimately acquainted with the

[1] *V.H.* XII. 48. Also by Plutarch, *Vit. Alex.*

[2] Yet he had predecessors, for he found there a Christian church said to have been founded by St Bartholomew, owning a Hebrew text of St Matthew's Gospel. Eusebius, *E.H.* V. 10.

[3] *Stromat.* III. 194, ed. Dindorf.

doctrines of Gautama. Clement distinguishes clearly between Buddhist and Brahmin,—Sarmanae and Brachmanae. Earlier writers like Megasthenes confuse them. Archelaus of Carrha (278 A.D.) and St Jerome (340 A.D.) both mention Buddha (*Buddas*) by name and narrate the tradition of his virgin birth[1]. The Buddha story became gradually known in the West, until, by a coincidence hardly to be paralleled in literature, it was narrated, in the eighth century A.D. by John of Damascus as the life of a Christian saint. Under the guise of Saint Josaphat, Gautama the Bodhisattva found his way into the Christian Church, and was included in the Martyrology of Gregory XIII (1582)[2].

We must now turn our attention to the very interesting work of Bardesanes the Babylonian on the Indian Gymnosophists. This treatise was extensively used by Porphyry, and there can be little doubt that it was through Bardesanes, that Indian philosophy exercised so great an influence on the development of Neo-platonism. Two important passages from the lost work of Bardesanes have been preserved, each shewing

[1] The passages are given in McCrindle, *Ancient India*, pp. 184–5. Terebinthus, mentioned above, according to Archelaus, called himself the new Buddha, and said he was born of a virgin and brought up on a mountain by the angels !

[2] For *Barlaam and Josaphat* see Max Müller, *Selected Essays*, I. 500. For text, *Löeb Classical Library*, London, 1914, and for the growth of the legend, Jacobs, *Barlaam and Josaphat*, 1896.

a most remarkably intimate knowledge of India on the part of the writer. His informant is stated to have been one Sandanes, Sandales, Dandamis or Damadamis, an Indian who came with an embassy to Syria to welcome the Emperor Elagabalus to the throne in 218 A.D. The first of these passages is to be found in the treatise Περὶ ἀποχῆς τῶν ἐμψύχων already referred to[1]. It begins by distinguishing carefully between the Brahmins,—a hereditary priesthood, descended from a common ancestry, and the Sarmanes, or Buddhists, who are drawn from all classes. The Brahmin, he says, is not even subject to the king, and pays no tribute. He lives in the mountains or by the Ganges, as a solitary recluse, and devotes his time to solitary meditation and the service of the gods. The Sarmanes were quite different in their habits. They were drawn from all castes, and when they took their vows, they went to the village magistrate and made a declaration disposing of their goods. The candidate was then shaved, put on the robe of his order, and joined the fraternity. His wife went back to her relatives, and the state took charge of his children. Of life in a Buddhist monastery, the following account of Bardesanes is extremely interesting, and should be compared with that given by Hiuen Tsiang, the Chinese traveller[2], of life in the great Nālandā monastery four

[1] *De Abstinentia*, IV. 17–18.

[2] *Life*, trans. Beal, III. 111.

centuries later: "Their houses and temples are founded by the king, and in them are stewards who receive a fixed allowance from the state for the support of the inmates of the monastery, consisting of rice, bread, fruit, and herbs. When the monastery bell rings, all the strangers withdraw, and the monks enter and offer prayer. Prayer over, the bell is again rung, and the attendants give each monk a bowl of food, for two never eat out of the same dish. The bowl contains rice, but if anyone wants a variety of food, vegetables and fruits are added. Dinner is soon over, and the monks return to their several avocations. They are not allowed to marry or possess property. Both they and the Brahmins are held in such high esteem that the king himself will come and ask for their prayers and their counsel in times of emergency and danger." The writer then goes on to describe the practice of self-immolation, which, though forbidden by Gautama, had become increasingly common among Buddhist ascetics.

The second passage, preserved for us by Stobaeus[1], is even more striking. After describing a system of Trial by Ordeal in which water was employed, somewhat as mentioned by Hiuen Tsiang, the writer goes on to the following remarkable description of a rock-temple. "The Indian ambassadors told me further that there was a large natural cave in a very high mountain almost

[1] *Physica*, I. 56, ed. Gaisford.

in the middle of the country. Herein was a statue ten or twelve cubits high, standing upright, with its hands folded crosswise. And the right half of its face was that of a man, and the left half that of a woman. In like manner the right hand and right foot,—in a word, the whole of the right side,—were male, and the left female, and the spectator was wonderstruck at the combination, when he saw how indissolubly the two dissimilar halves coalesced into a single body. On the right breast was engraved the sun and on the left the moon, and on the arms a host of angels (*devas*), the sky, mountains, rivers and seas, plants and animals, and all the world contains." After going on to say that this statue had been given by the chief god to his son at the creation of the world, Bardesanes adds that it was made of a very hard substance resembling wood, but proof against rot. Probably this was teak. On the head of the statue sat a god, as if on a throne, and the sweat ran down the statue in the hot season almost to the ground, so that the attendant Brahmins had to cool it with their fans. Then comes another curious passage. "In the depths of the cave, far behind the statue, is a long dark passage, and here, say the Indians, the devotees advance with lighted torches till they come to a door. Out of the door water gushes and forms a pool at the far end of the cave. All who desire to prove themselves must pass through the door. To those who have led a pure life the door opens readily, and they find within a clear, sweet fountain, the source of the pool without. But the wicked strive in vain to push past the door, for it closes fast upon them."

There is little doubt that we have in this passage a description of one of the great Hindu rock-temples of the Deccan—Elephanta, Ajantā, or Kāṇheri[1]. Sandanes, the informant of Bardesanes, probably came from the Deccan. In the *Periplus*[2], a certain Sandares or Sandanes is mentioned, probably Sundara Śātakarṇi. This Sandanes was therefore probably Sundara, a Śaka from the Deccan too. The androgynous image was no doubt Arddhanārīshvara, Śiva in his double aspect, and the god (or goddess) seated upon his head, the Ganges nestling in his matted locks. From this arose, perhaps, the legend of the "streams of sweat" flowing down the statue. The curious passage about the Door reminds us of a similar test said to be applied to candidates in the cave-temple at the Eleusinian mysteries and refers, no doubt, to some forgotten esoteric rite.

Of other notices of India (passing over the purely fictitious account given by Philostratus of the wanderings of that prince of impostors, Apollonius of Tyana) we may select for mention a little pamphlet of the fifth century on the *Nations*

[1] Burgess (*Elephanta*, p. 20, 1871 edn.) says that Bardesanes is describing the gigantic image at Elephanta which stands in the chapel on the left of the shrine of the Trimurti.

[2] *Periplus*, § 52.

of India, included in the *Romance History of Alexander* of the Pseudo-Kallisthenes[1]. The writer mentions having visited Southern India. There he was the guest of Moses, bishop of Adule, no doubt a Nestorian prelate. It is interesting to observe this early reference to the Christian Church in Southern India. He was deterred by the great heat from going far inland, but a friend of his, a Theban scholar, had shewn greater courage, and gave the writer some miscellaneous and not very accurate information about what he had seen. He visited Ceylon and was falsely informed that the king of that island was overlord of South India. He was told about the Laccadives, a group of "thousands of islands" (*Laksha dvīpa*), where the coconut was plentiful, and he observed that pork was never eaten in the East. He learnt that the pepper of Southern India was collected by the *Bisadae,* stunted men with large heads. These are the *Besatae* of the *Periplus*[2], a name contemptuously given by the Indians to the aboriginal tribes, derived from *vishāda,* dullness[3]. Of the Brahmins, the writer recounts the usual stories, with no novel or interesting particulars.

We now come to the last voyage of the ancient world to visit India. Kosmas Indikopleustes, a monk of the sixth century A.D. travelled down the Red Sea, and took ship to India and Ceylon.

[1] McCrindle, *Ancient India,* p. 178.

[2] § 65.

[3] See p. 123, *supra.*

The eleventh book of his *Christian Topography* gives an account of his experiences. His narrative resembles in many respects that of the writer referred to above. Like him, Kosmas found Christianity making good headway in Ceylon and South India. In Ceylon was a "Persian," *i.e.* Nestorian, Church, with a ritual of its own and a presbyter and deacon appointed in Persia. In the pepper country of Male (Malabar) was another, and a third as far north as Kalyan, with a Persian bishop. Christianity was spreading rapidly in Persia, Baktria, and Turkestan, and even in Sokotra, as Kosmas learnt from travellers, was a bishopric with a large following. In the northern part of India the White Huns already ruled, but the trade ports still prospered[1]. Of these Kosmas especially notices Sindu (the Indus[2] mouth), Orathra (Surāshṭra), Kalyān, Sibor (Simylla or Chaul), Male (Malabar), Mangaroutha (Mangalore), and the Pepper-country. Next, he says, comes Ceylon, and then China. China did a flourishing trade with India in silk, aloes, cloves and sandalwood, and beyond it, says Kosmas, lies a vast expanse of sea. It is interesting to notice how the knowledge of China had increased since the days of Ptolemy. A century after this, we find Hiuen Tsiang sailing back to China *viâ* Sumatra by a regular route. Ceylon had in

[1] Their king was named Gollas.

[2] Like the Pseudo-Kallisthenes he identifies the Indus and the Phison of Genesis!

the days of Kosmas attained great prosperity. As at the present moment, it was the great *entrepôt* of trade from China, India and the West. "Its position is central," says Kosmas, "and it is a great resort of ships from India, Persia and Ethiopia, and despatches many of its own." Its native name, he continues, is Sieladiba (*Siṅhala dvīpa*, the island of the Sinhalese or Lion people, whence the modern Ceylon), but the Indians call it Tapropane (*Tāmraparṇī*). It had two kings,—probably the Sinhalese king of Anurādhapura, and the Tamil ruler of the north,—and these two monarchs were frequently at war with one another. The Sinhalese monarch possessed a gigantic sapphire[1], "as large as a pine-cone, fire-coloured, and flashing far and wide in the sunshine, a matchless sight." It was placed in a temple which stood on an eminence. This famous jewel was no fiction upon the part of Kosmas. Hiuen Tsiang, a century later, writes of it: "Every night, when the sky is clear, and without clouds, can be seen at a great distance the glittering rays of the gem placed on the top of the *stūpa* of Buddha's tooth; its appearance is like that of a shining star in the midst of space[2]." Marco Polo had heard of it, but calls it a ruby.

Kosmas repeats a story, already told by Pliny, of how a Persian and a Roman trader arrived simultaneously at one of the Ceylon ports. They

[1] Ὑάκινθος. Perhaps *amethyst*.

[2] *Life of Hiuen Tsiang*, trans. Beal, IV. 134.

were received in audience by the Sinhalese monarch. The Persian talked volubly of the greatness of his country, but the Roman was silent. Then the king turned to the Roman and said, "Have you nothing to say?" The Roman, for reply, handed him a Roman *aureus* and bade him compare it with the Persian *drachma*. When the king contrasted the finely stamped gold coin of the Roman with the rough silver one of the Sassanian dynasty, he at once recognised the superiority of Rome as a trading nation. In Pliny's version[1], a freedman of Claudius, Annius Plocamus by name, who farmed the Red Sea revenues, was carried out to sea by a gale and landed at Hippuri (Kudremale, in the gulf of Manār). Here he was detained and convinced the Sinhalese, of the greatness of Rome by shewing them the uniformity of weight and workmanship of the coins in his possession. Kosmas includes in his account of the East a description of the animals and plants which he had come across, and he often gives them, very accurately, their Indian names. Amongst the animals enumerated are the rhinoceros, the ox deer, the giraffe, the wild ox, the musk deer, the hog deer, the hippopotamus, and the unicorn (which he truthfully owns he never saw, "but

[1] *N.H.* VI. 22. The narrative seems hardly appropriate to the days of Kosmas when Roman trade was fast dying out, owing to the destruction of the Empire of the West and the rivalry of the Sassanians. It had become a stock story, and was no doubt told in many forms.

only statues in the royal palace of Ethiopia"). Among "fishes," the seal, dolphin, and tortoise. Among plants, the coconut palm, and the pepper plant.

The long night of the Middle Ages was now settling down upon the Western world. The Neo-Sassanian Empire, with its great Persian renaissance, had manned a fleet which was fast sweeping the Roman vessels from Eastern waters. In 364 A.D., the first fatal step in the downfall of Rome had been taken, when the Empire was divided. In 410 came the Goths, and fifty years later the mightiest kingdom the world has ever seen had ceased to be. Yet even then Alaric's demand for "three thousand pounds of pepper" as part of the ransom of Rome, shewed that Eastern luxuries still found their way in vast quantities to the Imperial city. The Roman coins[1] found in South India tell their own tale. After Septimius Severus (211 A.D.), they dwindle rapidly, though there is a single hoard belonging to the days of Arcadius and Honorius (395 A.D.). No later coins of Western Emperors have been unearthed. Trade with the Eastern Empire, in spite of Persian rivalry, struggled feebly on, and a few scattered specimens of the time of Anastasius (491 A.D.) and Justinus (518 A.D.) are recorded. The latest coin found in Ceylon belongs to the

[1] For this and much other valuable information in this chapter, I am indebted to Mr R. Sewell's exhaustive article on *Roman Coins found in India* (*J.R.A.S.* 1904, p. 591).

reign of Honorius. The latest recorded Eastern embassy to Constantinople reached that city in 530 A.D.[1]

APPENDIX I

CEYLON IN THE CLASSICS

Besides the account given of Ceylon by Kosmas Indikopleustes, there are several notices of that island in the classics. Onesikritus, the pilot of Alexander, starts the legend that it was 5000 *stadia* long,—625 miles. Its actual length is 271½ miles. Strabo, Ptolemy, Pliny, and the writer of the *Periplus* repeat this, and often further exaggerate it. Pliny's account is the fullest. It was seven days sail, he says, from the country of the Prasii (*i.e.* the Bengal ports), but the coast is treacherous and unsafe in the south-west monsoon. The sailors take birds to guide them to shore when out of sight of land. This, we have seen, is an old Buddhist custom. Pliny then goes on to tell the story of the freedman of Annius Plocamus who was wrecked on the coast, and captivated the Sinhalese king by shewing him Roman coins. The monarch then sent an embassy, headed by one Rachia (*Rājā*) to Claudius. This Rachia said that his father had often gone to trade with the Seres, beyond the Himalayas, where the "silent barter" of malobathrum and other goods went on, as described by the author of the *Periplus*. But as Pliny says that the Seres had "yellow hair and blue eyes," it has been thought that he means the Cheras, a fair race living in the Mysore district[2]. Pliny says the capital of Ceylon is Palaesimundus (perhaps *Palaisimanta*)[3] a large city which may be Anurādhapura. He speaks of a great lake called

[1] Johannes Malala, 477, *apud* McCrindle, *Ancient India*, p. 212.

[2] Kennedy, *J.R.A.S.* 1904, p. 360 ff.

[3] Also in Ptolemy.

Megisba, which may be one of the huge tanks, like Tissa Wĕwa, of the Sinhalese monarchs. But he supposes it to be 375 miles round! The rest of Pliny's account of Ceylon is a queer mixture of fact and fancy. The Sinhalese are depicted as an ideal race, living gentle, peaceful lives. The king is elected, and assisted by a council of thirty. The condemned criminal has a right of appeal to the people. All this panegyric, though quite untrue, may have been suggested by the gentle and peaceful nature of the Sinhalese, which, together with the influence of Buddhism, made Ceylon an unusually happy island. (See Emerson Tennant's *Ceylon* London, 1859, vol. I.)

APPENDIX II

THE ROMAN EMPERORS

Augustus	29 B.C.–14 A.D.
Tiberius	A.D. 14–37.
Caligula	A.D. 37–41.
Claudius................	A.D. 41–54.
Nero	A.D. 54–68.
Galba, Otho, Vitellius	A.D. 68–69.
Vespasian	A.D. 69–79.
Titus	A.D. 79–81.
Domitian	A.D. 81–96.
Nerva	A.D. 96–98.
Trajan	A.D. 98–117.
Hadrian	A.D. 117–138.
Antoninus Pius	A.D. 138–161.
Marcus Aurelius...........	A.D. 161–180.
Commodus	A.D. 180–193.
Septimius Severus, etc.	A.D. 193–211.
Caracalla	A.D. 211–217.
Macrinus	A.D. 217.
Heliogabalus	A.D. 218–222.

Alexander Severus	A.D. 222–235.
Maximinus The Gordians }	A.D. 235–244.
Philip	A.D. 244–249.
Decius	A.D. 249.
Gallus, Aemilianus	A.D. 249–253.
Valerian	A.D. 253–260.
Gallienus	A.D. 260–268.
Claudius	A.D. 268–270.
Aurelian	A.D. 270–275.
Tacitus	A.D. 275–276.
Probus	A.D. 276–282.
Carus	A.D. 282–283.
Carinus, Numerian	A.D. 283.
Diocletian	A.D. 284–305.
Constantius, etc.	A.D. 305–323.
Constantine I	A.D. 323–353.
Constantine II	A.D. 353–361.
Julian	A.D. 361–363.
Jovian	A.D. 363.

EMPERORS OF THE EAST

Valens	A.D. 364–379.	Marcian	A.D. 450–457.
Theodosius I	A.D. 379–395.	Leo I	A.D. 457–474.
Arcadius	A.D. 395–408.	Leo II.	A.D. 474.
Theodosius II	A.D. 408–450.		

Kuvera. (From an Indo-Greek sculpture)
(*By permission of the Curator, Lahore Museum*)

CHAPTER VIII

THE EFFECTS OF THE INTERCOURSE BETWEEN INDIA AND THE WEST

We have seen, in the preceding chapters of this book, that for a period of about a thousand years,—from the invasion of Darius to the sack of Rome by the Goths,—India was in more or less constant communication with the West. Had this long intercourse of nearly ten centuries any influence upon the development of the art, literature, or thought of either India or of the Greco-Roman world?

It has already been shewn that the intercourse between India and Greece, before the days of Alexander, was of an indirect nature. Indian goods reached the Mediterranean from Persian or Phoenician caravans; the Indian traders themselves never went further than Babylon or the mouth of the Red Sea. Greece had no direct communication with India. What she knew of India, she had learnt from Greeks in Persian employ, like Ktesias or Skylax. Of the great civilization of ancient India, its philosophy and religion, Greece knew—and cared—nothing. The Greeks were singularly indifferent to the literature or civilization of their contemporaries. They looked on them all as "barbarians," and treated them with equal contempt. It is extraordinary how little they found out about even their near neighbours, the Persians. Hence we may dismiss at once the theory that the Pythagorean philosophy, for instance, owes anything to India. It is curious, however, to notice how many points of resemblance there are between the mystical philosophy of the Orphic and Pythagorean schools, and Indian beliefs [1]. First and foremost, there is the doctrine of Metempsychosis (παλιγγενεσία). But this was a tenet neither of the earliest Greeks nor of the original Aryans of the Panjāb. Practically no traces of it are found in the Vedas, or in the poems of Homer. The Vedic hero, like the Homeric hero, goes to dwell in the Elysium of Yama, the proto-man, and returns no more to earth [2]. The belief in re-incarnation appears first in India in its most primitive form in the *Chāndogya Upanishad*. In Greece, it is first traced to the Orphic schools, who acquired it, we may suppose, in Thrace. It seems probable, in a word, that both Greeks and Indians acquired the doctrine from the primitive peoples with whom they came in contact, —the Greeks from the Thracians, the Aryans from

[1] See for the whole subject the exhaustive article *Pythagoras and Transmigration*, by A. B. Keith, in *J.R.A.S.* 1909, p. 569, with a full bibliography. This is the last word on the subject, and sums up all possible sources of information.

[2] *Ṛig Veda*, x. 14.

the prae-Aryan tribes of the Ganges valley. Once acquired, the doctrine naturally assumed the form it did, for it provides the most natural of solutions to the eternal questions of the destiny of the soul and the existence of evil. Thus we find in Plato (in the closing episode of the *Republic,* for instance), something which resembles very closely the doctrine of *karma,* or retribution, commonly held by all Hindu sects. Again, the Pythagorean "tabus" on wine, animal food, etc., remind the reader of Buddhism. But Pythagoras lived before Gautama, and the *ahiṃsā* doctrine of Buddhism, shared also by the Brahmins and Jains, was a later development. Gautama himself died of eating some tainted flesh, offered to him by a humble follower. Finally, we may ask why, if Pythagoras, Plato, or any other Greek philosopher before the days of Alexander, borrowed anything from India, we find no mention of the fact in contemporary Greek literature. There are stories about visits paid to Egypt by both Pythagoras and Plato, and there is nothing intrinsically improbable in this. But a journey to India, except under very unusual circumstances, was at that time almost a physical impossibility[1]. And Plato never mentions Indian philosophy, or India at all, in all his

[1] The story of a visit to the Brahmins is told by very late writers, such as Diogenes and Iamblichus, of more than one early philosopher. But there is not the slightest trace of this legend before the 2nd century A.D. It *never* occurs in contemporary literature.

writings. Herodotus says nothing of the Indian doctrine of transmigration, and in a single sentence, he casually remarks that "some Indians kill nothing that has life, but live on herbs[1]." Egypt, not India, was the source, if any, from which Greece borrowed her early philosophy. Herodotus tells us distinctly that the Egyptians were the first to propound the theory of the transmigration of the soul, after death, through a cycle of other lives[2]; and in a well-known passage of the *Laws* Plato talks of the Greeks as children compared to the Egyptians in knowledge. In a word, there is not a single reference in Greek literature before 328 B.C. which gives us the slightest reason for supposing that the Greeks knew of the existence of Indian philosophy at all. The Indians, on the other hand, were equally ignorant of the literature and civilization of Greece, and equally indifferent to any system of thought outside India. If they ever heard of the *Yavanas* (Pāṇini mentions them once), it was in a doubtful and vague way, probably because an occasional Greek, like Skylax of Karyanda, in the service of the Persians, visited the Panjāb. It is therefore with surprise that we find no less an authority than Burnet[3] writing that

[1] III. 100. Mention has already been made (Ch. II.), of one or two Indian stories which have found their way into Herodotus. But this does not affect the argument.

[2] II. 123. Nor did this doctrine come through Egypt from India. Egypt is centuries older than India.

[3] *Early Greek Philosophy*, p. 21. The chief supporter of the theory is von Schröder, *Pythagoras und die Inder* (1884).

"everything points to the conclusion that Indian philosophy came from Greece." The resemblances, superficially very striking, are often, on thorough investigation, found to be far less complete than they appear to be at first sight. As for the theory of Metempsychosis, it has been found to exist among many early races. The Celts, for instance, believed in it, as Julius Caesar discovered[1]. The legend said to be inscribed upon king Arthur's tomb

> Hic iacet Arthurus, *Rex quondam Rexque futurus*,

is one of the many traces, often overlaid by Christianity, of the original Celtic belief in this doctrine. Yet no one will be disposed to contend that the Celts borrowed it from the Greeks. It is far more probable that the belief was a common one among early peoples, and held by Celts and Thracians alike, long before the Greeks acquired it.

India was totally unaffected by Greece before the days of Alexander. Between the two countries lay the unsurmountable barriers of vast seas, deserts, mountains and hostile nations; these alone would have made intercourse impossible, without the obstacles of an alien tongue and mutual exclusiveness. On the other hand, as we have already seen, there had been a long and continuous intercourse between India and the great nations of Asia Minor. Yet, as we have stated in a previous chapter, the traces of this contact are

[1] *De Bello Gallico*, VI. 14. 5.

on the whole doubtful and comparatively insignificant. India may owe to her intercourse with the Semitic races her earliest script, perhaps too her calendar, her system of weights and measures, and some Purāṇic legends. Persia, of course, was in close contact with India for nearly two centuries, and the Panjāb was a Persian satrapy for that period. Indian architecture appears to have assimilated a great many Persian forms, but on the whole, the effects of the contact were surprisingly few. Indian literature could find nothing to borrow from her great neighbour.

We now come to the invasion of Alexander. Alexander himself, owing to his untimely death, had no direct influence upon India, and in the great upheaval which followed, the Macedonian power in the Panjāb, with its colonies and wharfs and harbours, was swept away in a moment. But the contact between East and West, once established, was never entirely severed. Alexander's followers, in their numerous narratives of their great adventure, first informed their countrymen of the beliefs and customs of the East. Greeks heard for the first time of Brahmins and Śramaṇas, people with superstitions and beliefs strangely like their own. Besides considerable bodies of settlers who remained behind in the Panjāb, there was the great Greek colony at Bakṭra, on the highroad to India. At the same time, the Maurya Emperors, thanks to the extraordinarily enlightened policy of the great founder of their dynasty, kept in close touch with their Greek neighbours. Yet here, again, it is remarkable how little the Greek spirit influenced India. Hellenism, which affected profoundly the whole of Western Asia and even Egypt, stopped short at the Hindu Kush, in spite of the presence of a Greek *rāṇī* at Pāṭaliputra and of the close and friendly relations existing between the Mauryas and their brother monarchs of Syria and Egypt. Chandragupta, who had spent his early days as an exile in the Panjāb, where Persian civilization had taken a strong hold on the country was imbued with Persian ideas. Of Greek culture he and his successors exhibit hardly a trace.

With the break up of the Maurya Empire, however, came a fresh foreign invasion of North-Western India. Disturbances in Central Asia drove the Baktrian Greeks south of the Hindu Kush, where they established a kingdom with its capital at Sāgala, afterwards splitting up into a series of petty principalities. These Greek principalities, after enjoying considerable power for a time, were succeeded, as we have already seen, firstly by Skythian or Śaka chiefs, and finally by the Kushān tribe, who quickly absorbed all the petty states of the Panjāb and established a vast Empire, with its capital at Peshāwar, stretching from the Oxus to the Ganges.

It is an interesting and still unsolved problem, how far the Baktrian Greeks actually affected the civilization of North-Western India. Probably the results of their brief reign were not great. They were a mere handful, and their coins shew that they were rapidly absorbed by the surrounding population. The coins of Demetrius, for instance, are purely Hellenic; those of Menander a curious compromise between Greece and India. Again, there is evidence that the Baktrian Greeks very largely adopted the religion of their neighbours, and they could scarcely do this until they had become Hindus in all but name. The conversion of Menander to Buddhism is as dramatic as that of Aśoka. In the Nāsik caves is a *leṇa* owned by "Indrāgnidatta a Yonaka from Dattamitra (*Demetria*) in the north." In the Kārla caves are several votive offerings from Greeks, some of them being from Benākaṭakā near Nāsik[1]. Most remarkable of all is the curious inscription on the Garuda pillar from Besnagar, recording that it is the work of "Heliodorus son of Dion, a Greek envoy[2] from Takshasilā, sent by the Mahārājā Antialkidas[3]." From these inscriptions it will be seen that the Greeks in the Panjāb and in Western India rapidly became converts to Hinduism and Buddhism, and were so little distinguishable from their neighbours that they even took Hindu names. Further than this, the solitary monument of Baktrian architecture,—the Besnagar pillar referred to above,—is purely Indo-Persian in type. No trace of Menander's famous capital at Sāgala has survived,

[1] *Bombay Gazetteer*, XVIII. Ins. No. 7 & 10. Rapson, *Coins of the Āndhras*, Int. XXIX., XLVII.

[2] *Yona-dūta* (?)

[3] *J.R.A.S.* 1909, p. 1092.

but there is no reason to suppose that it was in the Greek style[1]. It is probable, however, that a corrupt Greek was spoken among these half caste settlers, and was perhaps the *lingua franca* of the Greek, Indo-Parthian, and Śaka tribes at that time. The Indo-Parthians had an additional reason to use Greek, as that was the court language of Parthia. They also used the Greek names for the months[2].

With the Kushāns we come upon different ground. These great rulers, about whom we know only too little, built up a vast Empire, comprising a variety of nationalities. In the Panjāb were semi-Asiatic Greeks, Parthians, Skythians, Hindus. In Afghanistan and Baktria, besides the remnants of the older Skythian and Iranian settlers, were Greeks, Parthians, and their own countrymen from Central Asia. Besides this, the Kushān monarchs were in intimate touch with the Roman power in Asia Minor. With the establishment of the Roman Empire, traders began to come to Western India in great numbers, both by land and sea. The Roman Emperors pursued a forward policy in Asia, and Trajan pushed forward to within six hundred miles of the Kushān frontiers. It was probably in his time that intercourse

[1] Sir J. H. Marshall, however, traces the Gandhāra sculptures to the workmanship of Baktrian Greeks, *not*, as is usually supposed, to workmen imported by Kanishka (*J.R.A.S.* 1909, p. 1060 ff.).

[2] *Panemus* in the Taxila copperplate inscription of Patika.

between India and the Roman power in Asia Minor reached its height. More than one embassy had been sent to the Roman Emperors from the Kushān monarchs. One which reached Rome in the days of Trajan was treated by him with the utmost courtesy and distinction. The cosmopolitan nature of the Empire of the Kushān kings is shewn by their coins. Kadphises I imitates the bronze and copper coinage of Augustus[1]. Kadphises II strikes an *aureus* in imitation of the Roman coin,—probably re-striking the actual Roman *aureus*[2]. Some of the coins of Kanishka represent a most curious blending of nationalities and creeds: the king appears in Turki dress, standing by a fire-altar, and the coin bears a polyglot inscription in Greek letters *shaonanoshao Kaneshki Koshano,* "Kanishka the Kushān, King of Kings[3]." The use of the Persian phrase *Shahan Shah,* Βασιλεὺς *βασιλέων*, is very curious. So is the employment of þ to represent *sh,* a sound which finds no expression in the Greek alphabet. These coins were, no doubt, like those bearing the image of NANAIA[4] (Anaitis, the

[1] Gardner, *Cat. Greek and Scythic Coins in B.M.* XXV. 5.

[2] *Ibid.* 6–10.

[3] *Ibid.* XXVI. 4–19. Gardner, of course, fails to see that þ = *sh.* This was first discovered, I think, by Burgess, and propounded in the *Indian Antiquary*. It may be the old *San* letter revived.

[4] *Ibid.* XXVI. 3. etc. See also Stein, *Zoroastrian Deities on Indo-Scythian Coins* (*Babylonian and Oriental Record,* I. 133).

tutelary goddess of Balkh), and other Iranian deities, struck for use in the Iranian parts of the Kushān Empire. Another typical coin of the time bears a *male* figure of the moon and the superscription ΣΑΛΗΝΗ [1]. The most important achievement of the Kushāns, however, from our present point of view, was the importation of a large number of Greek sculptors from Asia Minor, to decorate the Buddhist monasteries, *stūpas*, and other religious buildings which were erected all over the Peshāwar district after the conversion of Kanishka [2]. These sculptors appear to have settled down in the Panjāb, and their work, at first purely Greek, becomes much more tinged, as time goes on, with Indian ideas, particularly those of the indigenous Buddhist school of Sānchi and Barhut. Remains of this school have been found extensively in the Gandhāra district, from which they have received their name. The remarkable casket, containing relics of the Buddha, found at Peshāwar in 1908, bears an inscription to the effect that it is the work of "Agesilaus, overseer of works at Kanishka's *vihāra*." In itself, this curious reliquary is of little merit. It is shaped like a Greek lady's jewel-casket, and the figures are roughly and clumsily executed [3]. About the fourth century A.D., the Kushān power waned and disappeared. The

[1] *Ibid.* XXVI. I.

[2] This, however, is not Marshall's view, as we have already stated.

[3] Marshall in *J.R.A.S.* 1909, p. 1060 ff.

sceptre now returned to the great indigenous dynasty of the Guptas. Under the Gupta monarchs, a splendid literary and artistic renaissance set in, strongly nationalistic in character, and except perhaps in some coin-issues, Greco-Roman influence entirely disappears. The rise of the Sassanian Empire also placed a barrier which cut off all direct communication between Roman Asia and the East. Intercourse between the Roman world and the East was now almost entirely confined to the great port of Alexandria, to which Indians flocked in ever-increasing numbers. The Roman traders who resorted to Southern India at this time, and even settled at Madura and other places, came for mercantile purposes only, and had apparently no effect whatever upon literature or art.

Having thus summarized in general terms the nature of the intercourse between India and the Greco-Roman world, we must seek more specifically its results. As regards Indian art, we may at once say that in the matter of *coinage*, Indians learnt everything from the West. Coinage never appealed to the Hindu craftsman very strongly, though very occasionally,—as in the case of the life-like portraits of Kanishka, and the beautiful and graceful types of the versatile Samudra Gupta [1], —a fine result is achieved. The Indians were usually content either to imitate foreign coins, generally the Roman *aureus*, or to restrike them. In the south of India they took the simpler course

[1] *J.R.A.S.* 1889, Pl. I. 4 and 5.

of importing Roman specie wholesale[1]. Not much can be said for the purely native coins of the Āndhras, Chālukyas or Pāṇḍyas.

Besides the Kushāns, the Śaka, Indo-Parthian and the Kshaharāta princes issued coins which are more or less a compromise between Greco-Roman and Oriental ideas. Those of Nahapāna are a clever imitation of the Greek style applied to realistic portraiture[2]. Before Alexander, punch-marked coins were alone issued in India, though Persian and Athenian coins were in circulation in the satrapy of the Panjāb[3].

As regards art, we must obviously look to Gandhāra for the chief source of Greco-Roman influence upon India. These sculptures, as we have already seen, were probably the work of craftsmen imported from Syria. These craftsmen were not, of course, artists of a high order. None of their productions shews any inspiration or any outstanding merit, and Syrian art at the time was decadent. It appears likely that these artists settled in the Panjāb, as their productions, purely Greek at first, become, as time goes on, more and more deeply tinged with Indian influence. The latest work of the Gandhāra school is a compromise between Greek and early Buddhist art. It has

[1] The names of the chief coins have passed into Indian vernaculars. *Dramma* (mod. *dām*), is δραχμή. *Dīnāra* is denarius. *Statīra* is stater.

[2] Barnett, *Antiq. of India*, v. 2.

[3] Rapson, *Indian Coins*, in *Grundriss*, §§ 7–9.

been the fashion of late to abuse the Gandhāra sculptures roundly. This is not altogether fair. They possess, of course, nothing like the beauty or vigour of the graceful and powerful work of the Gupta period, but many of them are by no means devoid of charm and interest. They are a lively commentary on the life of Gautama and the *Jātaka* legends. The Gandhāra sculptors were the first to portray the Master as a human being. The earlier Buddhist sculptors, with puritanical abhorrence of idolatry, merely indicate his presence by symbols such as footmarks (*pāduka*), the wheel, or the umbrella. The conventional figure of the Master in modern Hīnayāna Buddhism of to-day, shews in the halo, the arrangement of the drapery, and the treatment of the hair, traces of borrowing from Gandhāra. The Corinthian pillars which appear on some of the friezes, with the figures placed among the foliage of the capital, and finished with stucco, resemble Roman work of the third century [1]. These pillars are ornamental, of course, not structural. Kanishka's buildings were, no doubt, purely Indian in type, but being made principally of wood and brick, in Indian fashion, they have almost entirely vanished. There is no reason to suppose that India was in any way influenced by Greek architecture. By 400 A.D., if not earlier, the Gandhāra school appears to have been completely extinct.

[1] This degraded workmanship first appears in the Baths of Caracalla (217 A.D.).

We now turn to Indian literature. A claim has been made[1] that Indian drama, if not Indian philosophy, owes a great deal to the drama of Greece. Many curious resemblances between the two have been pointed out. The *vidūshaka* and the *viṭa*, have been compared to the Parasite and the Pimp of the New Attic Comedy. The *Nāṭya Śāstra* of Bharata lays down as one of the canons of the drama that the number of persons appearing upon the stage should be limited to five. Indian like Greek drama, avoids the portrayal of violent or unseemly actions. The "Greek curtain" (*Yavanikā*) was used, and *Yavanī*, Greek girls, appear as the attendants upon royal persons. At Rāmgarh, a small Greek amphitheatre has been unearthed[2]. The *Toy Cart*[3] is compared by critics to plays of the type of the New Attic Comedy. Again, the passage of Chrysostom is quoted, wherein he states that "it is said that the poetry of Homer is sung by the Indians, who had translated it into their own language and modes of expression, so that even these Indians are not unacquainted with the woes of Priam

[1] Chiefly by Weber (*Sansk. Lit.* p. 224, etc.), Windisch (*Greek Influence on Indian Drama*), and Von Schröder(*Indiens Lit. und Cultur*). The opposite view is held by Sylvain Lévi (*Théâtre Indien*), and Rapson (Art. *Drama,* in Hastings' *Dict. Religion and Ethics*). For a complete bibliography see Macdonell, *History of Sanskrit Literature,* Bibliographical note to Ch. XVI.

[2] Bloch, *Annual Report, Arch. Surv. Ind.* 1903–4, p. 123 ff.

[3] *Mṛicchakaṭikā.*

and the weeping and wailing of Andromache and Hecuba, and the heroic feats of Achilles and Hector, so potent was the influence of what one man had sung[1]." Plutarch attributes to Alexander's invasion the fact that the Gedrosian read Homer, Euripides and Sophokles. A similar statement is made by Aelian[2].

But here, as in the case of Greek and Indian philosophy, the resemblances are not so close as they appear to be at first sight. On the whole, the Indian drama, with its neglect of the unities, its mixture of prose and verse, comedy and tragedy, resembles the severe Greek tragedy as little as a florid Indian temple resembles the Parthenon. The "Greek curtain" is certainly not borrowed from the Greek stage, for there the curtain was not used[3]. The presence of Greek girls as royal attendants shews they were commonly found in Rājās' harems[4], but this has no bearing upon the question of Hellenic influence on the drama. The supposed resemblances are really confined to a single play, the *Toy Cart*; they are not discernible in the other dramas of Kālīdāsa and Bhavabhūti. This seems to shew that the supposed Greek influence in the Indian drama, if it exists at all, is due to the Hellenic element in

[1] *Orations*, LIII. 554. [2] *V.H.* XII. 48.

[3] It is a curtain *made of Greek stuff* in all probability,—nothing more.

[4] They are mentioned among the imports of Barygaza, (Εὐειδεῖς παρθένοι ἐς παλλακίαν, *Periplus*, 49). See p. 117.

North-Western and Western India in the first two centuries after Christ, rather than to the later contact with Alexandria. This appears to be the most plausible theory, if we suppose the *Toy Cart* to be an early play. But was Greek ever talked sufficiently in the Panjāb to make a Greek drama intelligible to an Indian, or semi-Indian audience? The point seems very doubtful. The Greek on the coins,—except in the case of the Baktrian kings,—is so corrupt that we are almost forced to conclude that if spoken at all, it was a barbarous jargon, bearing only the remotest resemblance to classical Greek. It may, indeed, have been a dead language, only surviving on the coins along with other traces of imitation from foreign models [1]. Menander and his courtiers may have enjoyed a Greek comedy at Sāgala. It is highly improbable that Kanishka ever did. Chrysostom certainly asserts that this was the case. His accounts of India in other Orations are, however, mere poetical fables. He knew little about India. Is his story about the knowledge of Homer in India merely the result of some vague account, communicated to him by an Indian in Alexandria,

[1] Not a single Greek *inscription* has been unearthed. Even Greeks use Prākrit. This is significant enough. On the other hand, Sir J. H. Marshall found at Peshāwar a piece of Gandhāra pottery representing a scene which he considers to be unmistakably from the *Antigone*. He thinks this is evidence for the acting of Greek plays in the Panjāb. *J.R.A.S.* 1909, pp. 1060–1.

of the *Rāmāyaṇa* or *Mahābhārata*[1], some episodes of which resemble the *Iliad* to a certain degree? The assertion that an author as late as Kālīdāsa had read not only Menander but Plautus seems to be absolutely unwarranted[2]. If the Indian drama was actually affected by Hellenistic influences in the Baktrian or Kushān period, we may trace to the same time the supposed debt of Indian to Greek medicine. Charaka, said to have been the court physician of Kanishka, prescribes rules for the Indian doctor which resemble very minutely the oath which the Greek physician, according to Hippokrates, had to take upon entering on his duties. The Indian theory of the three humours has been also traced to Greek sources[3].

It is, however, in one respect only that we can definitely ascribe any real debt on the part of India to Greece. This is in the science of astronomy[4]. The Indians frankly acknowledged their

[1] The *Mahābhārata*, the present recension of which is about 300 A.D., contains some Greek words, *e.g.* *saptantrī vīṇā* (ἑπτάτονος φόρμιγξ) III. 134. 14; *trikoṇa* (τρίγωνος) XIV. 88. 32; *barbarān* (βάρβαρος) III. 51. 23. Greeks are mentioned II. 14. 4, III. 254. 18, XII. 207. 43. Romans are mentioned II. 51. 17. Greeks are called *sarvajñā* VIII. 45. 36, probably for their proficiency in astronomy.

[2] V. A. Smith, *Graeco-Roman Influence on the Civilization of Ancient India* (*J.R.A.S.* 1889).

[3] Hoernle, *Ancient Indian Medicine* (*J.R.A.S.* 1908, p. 997, 1909, p. 857 ff.).

[4] Kaye, in *J.R.A.S.* 1910, p. 759. Von Schröder, *Indiens Lit. und Cultur*. Barnett, *Antiquities of India*, Ch. VI. Weber, *Ind. Lit.* p. 247. Fleet attributes to this period the week of

indebtedness to Greek science in this respect: "The Yavanas are barbarians," writes the author of the *Gārgī Saṃhitā*, "yet the science of astronomy originated with them, and for this they must be reverenced like gods." There are five *Siddhāntas*, or Treatises, on astronomy, in medieval Sanskrit literature,—the *Paitāmaha*, the *Vāśishṭha*, the *Sūryya*, the *Pauliśa* and the *Romaka*. These frequently mention "*Romaka*" as a "famous city," and *Romaka* is also alluded to several times in the *Bṛihat Saṃhitā* and *Pañcha Siddhāntikā* of Varāhamihira[1]. This *Romaka* must be Alexandria, of course. The *Pauliśa Siddhānta* is based on the astronomical works of Paul of Alexandria (*circa* 378 A.D.). And Rome had ceased to exist as a centre of culture by the time of Varāhamihira (d. 587 A.D.). Further evidence may be found, if needed, in the fact that these writers all use the Greek names for the planets and the signs of the Zodiac instead of their regular Sanskrit appellations. Thus we have *Kriya* (Κριός, Aries), *Tāvuri* (Ταῦρος), *Jituma* (Δίδυμος), *Pāthona* (Παρθένος); *Āra* (Ἄρης), *Heli* (Ἥλιος), *Āsphiyit* (Ἀφροδίτη), *Himna* (Ἑρμῆς), and so on. Similarly

seven days, corresponding to the modern week in names of the days. This seems to me doubtful, the names of the days of the week only appearing very late indeed in Roman and Greek literature.

[1] *e.g. Romakākhyā prakīrtitā* in the *Sūryya Siddhānta*, *passim*. In the *Gārgī Saṃhitā* Alexandria is called *Yavanapura* and is taken as the meridian instead of Ujjain.

technical terms like *trikoṇa* (τρίγωνος), and *jāmitra* (διάμετρον), are freely employed[1]. The latter word occurs in Kālīdāsa[2], a contemporary of Varāhamihira. Varāhamihira also wrote a treatise on the *Hora Jñāna* or doctrine of Lunar Mansions. The term is no doubt borrowed from the Greek ὥρα (Latin *domus*) used in this sense by Firmicus Maternus 335 A.D.[3] On the other hand Europe borrowed, through the Arabs, a certain number of Sanskrit astronomical terms *e.g. aux*, apex, the Sanskrit *uchcha*. The Indian numerals, far less clumsy than the Greek and Roman ones, were also borrowed in the same way.

We now turn to the difficult and complicated question of Indian influence on the West. As we have already seen in the preceding chapters, this begins about the third century A.D., and was probably chiefly felt in Alexandria. Clement (d. 220 A.D.), is the first writer to shew any real knowledge of Eastern philosophy, in addition to the commonplaces repeated by successive writers since the time of Megasthenes. Porphyry, writing about 260 A.D., repeats more interesting details from the lost work of Bardesanes. Indians at the time were in the habit of visiting Alexandria and there seems little doubt that the Indian knowledge of Alexandrian astronomy was due to some of

[1] Von Schröder, *Indiens Lit. und Cultur*, p. 726.

[2] *Kumārasambhava*, VII. I.

[3] See Jacobi's pamphlet *De Horæ Originibus* (Bonn, 1872).

these visitors to the great centre of Greek learning. It certainly appears probable that Neo-platonism was affected by Oriental philosophy, though it is difficult to distinguish its borrowings from Pythagoreanism and Buddhism respectively. But perhaps the coincidences between Pythagorean and Buddhist beliefs lent them enhanced credence. Thus the tract Περὶ ἀποχῆς τῶν ἐμψύχων contains the famous description (already quoted) of a Buddhist monastery. Hence we may suppose that the doctrines it inculcates,—abstinence from flesh, subjection of the body by asceticism, and so on,—are derived from Oriental sources. In the case of the earlier Greek philosophers, we were driven to conclude that the resemblances between their tenets and those of the Indian sages were coincidences, because the evidence for intercourse was entirely lacking. In this case the links in the chain are supplied. In one point, we find a resemblance between Neo-platonic and Indian teaching, absent in Pythagoreanism. The Neo-platonist strives by meditation to free his soul from the body, and to attain union with the Supreme. This is the *Yoga* doctrine of Patañjali. Pythagoras, while teaching rebirth, "remembrance" (ἀνάμνησις), and abstention from flesh, says nothing about the end or aim—*Mukti* or Emancipation, which is the cardinal Hindu doctrine.

Did Christianity owe anything to Hindu and Buddhist thought? Many rash statements, which prove, on minute investigation, to be based on coincidences more or less remote, have been made upon this subject[1]. Thus the doctrine of the Logos, introduced into Christianity from Philo, superficially resembles the personification of *Vāch* 'Speech' as a goddess in the *Ṛig Veda*[2]. But there is no *Vāch doctrine, Vāch* being merely an unimportant abstraction. And moreover Philo borrowed his Logos doctrine from Heraklitus and not from the East at all. The immense popularity of asceticism, on the other hand, and the extravagant forms it assumed in the Thebaid, may very well be traced to the stories of the *Hylobioi* and *Sramanaioi* which are so prominent in patristic literature. The first of the great hermits was Paul of Alexandria, who fled to the Egyptian desert in 251 A.D. to escape the Decian persecution. His famous follower St Anthony died in 356 A.D. This is just the time when Indian influence in Alexandrian literature is most in evidence. Of course, monasticism was also practised among the Jews,—the Essenes of the Dead Sea and the Therapeutae in Egypt belong to the first century B.C. One cannot help wondering whether *relic-worship* (mentioned as we have seen by Clement as a Buddhist practice) and the use of the rosary, are not both Eastern survivals.

Of semi-Christian sects and heresies, and their

[1] To see how far wild speculation can take the untrained thinker, read Lillie, *India in Primitive Christianity* (1909).

[2] x. 125.

debt to the East, we have already spoken[1]. Manicheism is a strange farrago of Christian, Jewish, Persian, and Buddhistic ideas. Gnosticism, a far more serious and noble creed, together with its later offshoots, shews traces of both Hindu and Zarathustrian influence. Its doctrine of the plurality of Heavens is essentially Indian: its "three qualities" (πνευματικοί, ψυχικοί, ὑλικοί) resemble the "three *guṇas*" of the Sāṅkhya system. Origen's heretical belief in Metempsychosis must not be overlooked.

A great deal has been made, by Weber and others, of the supposed resemblances between the Kṛishṇa legend and the Gospel story[2]. Nanda, the foster-father of Kṛishṇa, goes up to Mathurā to pay his taxes (*kara*) to Kaṃsa; Kṛishṇa is born in a cow-shed (*gokula*); the wicked Kaṃsa, in order to slay him, massacres the infants of Mathurā; Kṛishṇa raises the son of a widow from the dead; Kubjā anoints him with precious ointment, and so forth. But these parallels (with the possible exception of the "Massacre of the Innocents") are vague and unsatisfactory, in spite

[1] Nestorianism, however, became the actual Christian church of India, though Nestorianism has no peculiarly Oriental affinities.

[2] See the *Vishṇu Purāṇa*, trans. Wilson, p. 503 ff. for the birth and childhood of Kṛishṇa. The raising of the widow's son only occurs in the late *Jaimini Bhārata*. The Vallabhas of Gujarat worship the Infant Kṛishṇa and his Mother. Much has been made of this curious coincidence, *e.g.* by Kennedy in *J.R.A.S.* 1907.

of the vast amount of ingenuity which has been expended on them. Still less convincing are the parallels between the Gospels and the *Bhagavad Gītā*, collected with such industry by Lorinser[1]. In the same way, Weber takes the incident in the *Mahābhārata* of the visit of Nārada and other Sages to the mysterious island of *Śvetadvīpa* or White Island, to be a poetical account of an actual visit on the part of some Indian travellers to Alexandria or Persia or some other Christian country. The description of the White Island is purely imaginary, and there is no reason to suppose that any reference to Christianity is intended in the remotest fashion[2]. Even less satisfactory are the supposed parallels between the life of Gautama and that of Christ. It is, however, probable that the striking resemblances which Lamaist ritual of to-day bears to Catholic ceremonies may be due to the influence of the Christian Church in Persia. These resemblances seem to be something more than coincidence. They startled the Abbé Huc when he visited Lhassa in 1842. "The crozier, the mitre, the chasuble, the cardinal's robe,...the double choir at the Divine Office, the chants, the

[1] *Die Bhagavad Gītā*, Breslau, 1869. Trans. in *Indian Antiquary*, 1873, p. 283. An able refutation is given in the introduction to Telang's translation of the *Gītā* in the *Sacred Books of the East*.

[2] The passage is in *Mahābhārata*, XII. 12. 702. Weber's views are in his *Indische Studien*, I. 400. See P. C. Ray's translation (Calcutta, 1891), VIII. 752.

exorcism, the censer with five chains, the blessing which the Llamas impart by extending the right hand over the heads of the faithful, the rosary, the celibacy of the clergy, their separation from the world, the worship of saints, the fasts, processions, litanies, holy water,—these are the points of contact which the Buddhists have with us[1]."

A few brief words on the remaining question of the influence of India upon Western literature must be added in conclusion. Here, again, we must beware of unwarranted assumptions, based upon coincidence. There is, however, good evidence for the steady migration of folk-tales from East to West, from the time of the *Jātaka* stories. Many Eastern legends have found their way into Europe, and may be found in the *Gesta Romanorum*, the *Decameron*, and other medieval collections. This was very largely due to the Arabs of Damascus, who translated much Sanskrit literature and transmitted it in this way to Europe. A typical instance are the famous fables of Bidpai or Pilpay[2]. They were translated from the Sanskrit *Pañcha Tantra* into Persian by Barzuyeh, in the time of Nushirvan, King of Persia. From Persian they were turned into Arabic by Abdalla ibn Mokaffa, at the court of Ibn Jāfar Almansūr at Bagdad. About the same time, at the neighbouring court

[1] Huc et Gabet, *Voyages*, I. 29.

[2] Benfey, *Pañcha Tantra*, Introduction (1859); *Bidpai*, ed. Keith Falconer (1885), Introduction; Sayce, *Science of Language* (1883), Ch. IX.

of Damascus, St John of Damascus also wrote *Barlaam and Josaphat*, which, as we have seen, contains numerous Buddhist stories and apologues. Thus the well-known story of the Three Caskets found its way into the *Merchant of Venice*. Thus, too, Chaucer was enabled to embody in his *Pardoner's Tale*, a Buddhist parable taken from the *Vedabbha Jātaka*[1]. On the whole subject, however, the words of a recent writer are worth remembering: "All these parallels prove nothing. In the first place, a large number of them can be considered parallels only by straining the sense of the term: and in the second place, they are the results of obviously independent though partially similar processes in the development of Greek and Sanskrit literature, and should be treated accordingly[2]."

[1] Skeat's *Oxford Chaucer* (1904), III. 443. Clouston, *Originals and Analogues*, Chaucer Society, 417.

[2] L. H. Gray in the *Encyclopedia of Religion and Ethics*, VI. 4. See also Tawney, *Journal of Philology*, XII. 121. F. Lacôte, *Essai sur Guṇādhya et le Bṛihatkathā*, Paris, 1908.

BIBLIOGRAPHY

(The following list does not pretend to be exhaustive, and editions are not specified. It contains, however, the principal works consulted in the preparation of the preceding pages, and may serve as a guide to the chief sources from which further information may be obtained.)

I. ANCIENT AUTHORS. **Arrian,** ed. Krüger. **Bohn,** *Standard Library* (translations of the principal classical authors). **Herodotus,** ed. and trans. Rawlinson. **McCrindle, J. W.,** *The Indika of Megasthenes and Arrian*: *Commerce and Navigation of the Erythrean Sea*: *Ptolemy's Geography of India*: *The Invasion of India by Alexander the Great* (Arrian, Q. Curtius, Diodorus, Plutarch, Justin): *Ancient India* (Herodotus, Strabo, Pliny, and later authors). **Müller, C.,** *Geographici Graeci Minores*. *Periplus Maris Erythraei*, ed. Fabricius: ditto trans. Schoff. **Pliny,** ed. Mayhoff. **Ptolemy,** ed. Müller and Fischer. **Strabo,** ed. Meineke.

II. INDIAN HISTORY, GEOGRAPHY, AND COMMERCE. **Bhandarkar, R. G.,** *Early History of the Deccan*. **Barnett,** *Antiquities of India*. **Beazley, C. R.,** *Dawn of Modern Geography*. **Bühler,** *Indian Studies* (1895). **Bunbury,** *Ancient Geography*. **Burgess,** *Elephanta*. **Cunningham, Sir A.** *Ancient Geography of India*: *Archaeological Survey of India*. **Dittenberger,** *Inscriptionum Graecarum Sylloge*. **Duff, M.,** *Chronology of India*. **Dutt, U. C.,** *Materia Medica of the Hindus*. **Hirth,** *China and the Roman Orient*. **Hoernle, R.,** *Ancient Indian Medicine* (*J.R.A.S.* 1898). **Kennedy, J.,** *Early Commerce of India with Babylon* (*J.R.A.S.* 1898). **Lassen,** *Indische Alterthumskunde*. **Lévi, S.,** *La Grèce et L'Inde d'après les documents indiens* (*Revue des études Grecques*, 1891). **Mukerji, R.,** *Indian Shipping*. **Oppert, Gustav,** *Ancient Commerce of India*. **Priaulx,** *Indian*

Travellers (*J.R.A.S.* 1861–2). **Rawlinson, H. G.,** *Baktria.* **Saint-Martin, V. de,** *Étude sur la Geographie Grecque.* **Smith, V. A.,** *Early History of India.* **Stein, Aurel,** *Ancient Geography of Kashmir: Sand Buried Cities of Khotan.* **Tennant, E.,** *Ceylon.* **Vincent,** *Commerce and Navigation of the Ancients.* **Yule,** *Marco Polo: Cathay and the Way Thither.* **Watt,** *Commercial Products of India.* **Wilson, H. H.,** *Ariana Antiqua.*

III. INDIAN LITERATURE, RELIGION, AND ART. **Bohlen,** *Altes Indien.* **Bournouf,** *Sciences des Religions.* **D'Alviella,** *Ce que l'Inde doit à la Grèce.* **Droysen,** *Hellenismus.* **Goldstücker,** *Pāṇini, His Place in Sanskrit Literature.* **Foucher,** *L'Art du Gandhāra.* **Hopkins, H.,** *India, Old and New: Religions of India: Great Epic of India.* **Jacobs, J.,** *Barlaam and Josaphat.* **Keith,** *Pythagoras and Transmigration* (*J.R.A.S.* 1909). **Kennedy, J.,** *The Child Krishna, Christ, and the Gujars* (*J.R.A.S.* 1907). **Leitner,** *Greek Influence on India* (Oriental Congress, 1880). **Lévi, S.,** *Théâtre Indien.* **Lorinser,** *Der Bhagavad Gītā.* **Macdonell,** *Vedic Index: History of Sanskrit Literature.* **Oldenburg,** *Ancient India.* **Rapson,** *Ancient India.* **Smith, V. A.,** *Graeco-Roman Influence on Ancient Indian Civilization: History of Fine Art in India and Ceylon.* **Tarn,** *Hellenism in Bactria* (*J.H.S.* 1902). **Telang,** *Bhagavad Gītā* (*S.B.E.* VIII.). **Weber,** *Indian Literature: Indische Skizzen: Die Griechen in Indien, etc.* **Windisch,** *Greek Influence on Indian Drama.* (Fifth Oriental Congress, Berlin, 1882.)

IV. NUMISMATICS. **Gardner,** *Catalogue of the Coins of Greek and Scythic Kings of Bactria and India in the British Museum.* **Rapson,** *Indian Coins: Coins of the Āndhras.* **Sewell,** *Roman Coins found in India* (*J.R.A.S.* 1904). **Smith, V. A.,** *Catalogue of Coins in the Indian Museum, Calcutta.* **Stein, Aurel,** *Zoroastrian Deities on Indo-Scythian Coins.* **Thurston,** *Catalogue of Coins in the Madras Museum.*

INDEX

[The letters ff. after an entry imply that references to the same subject occur on at least two immediately succeeding pages.]

Abdalla ibn Mokaffa 179
Abhīra 11
Abyssinia (*Itiopyavan*) 19, 92
acacia tree 126
Achilles 140, 170
Actium 101
Adad-Nirari IV. 8
Aden 1, 2, 10, 17, 94, 112
Āditya 139
Adulis (= Massowa) 91, 92
Aegidii (?Angidīva or Goa) 119
Aelana (= Ezion Geber, *q.v.*) 90
Aelian 49, 107, 170
Aelius Gallus 104
Aemilianus 154
Afghanistan 69, 163
Africa 14, 19, 98, 99
African baobab, the 14
Agatharchides 94, 113
Agathokleia 86
Agathokles 76, 86
Agesilaus 165
aghil (*ahal*) 14
Agnimitra 81
Airrhadii 133
Ajantā 9, 146
Akaba (*also called* Aelana *and* Ezion Geber) 10
Ākāśa (ether) 61
Akesines, R. 34, 78
Akkad 16
Akkadian tongue, the 2
Alaric 102, 151
Alasanda, island of 78
Alexander the Great 16, 19, 24, 29, 33 ff., 59, 88 ff., 117, 155, 159, 160, 167
Alexander, a trader 132
Alexander Severus 154
Alexandria 15, 69, 88 ff., 95 ff., 106, 111, 130, 137, 138, 140, 141, 171, 173, 174, 178
Alexandria-on-Indus (Alasanda of the Yonas) (= Ucch) 34, 38, 72
almug trees (*valgu*) 11
Amritsar district 59
'Αμύκτηρες 65
Amyntas 86
Anahid (=Anaitis) 23, 70, 72, 164
Āndhra princes 84, 167
Andromache 140, 170
Angidīva 119
Angrammes (*and see* Xandrames) 33
Angria 112
Annam 130
Annius Plocamus 106, 111, 113, 150, 152
Anthropophagi 26, 27
Antialkidas 77, 86, 162
Antigonus 38
Antimachus 74, 76, 86
Antioch 1, 9, 108, 130
Antiochus I (*Soter*) 93, 100; II (*Theos*) 100; III (*Megas*) 70, 74, 92, 100; IV (*Epiphanes*) 48, 100; V (*Eupator*) 100
Antipodes of Ktesias, the 27
'Αντίποδες (='Οπισθοδάκτυλοι) 66
Antonines, the 103
Antoninus Pius 153
Antonius, king of Syria 130
Antun 130
Anupshahr 42
Anurādhapura 149, 152
Apamea 128
Apollo Bunder (*Pālvā Bandar*) 119
Apollodorus of Artemita 78
Apollodotus II 72, 73, 76, 77, 86, 116
Apollonius of Tyana 146
Apollophanes 86
Apologus 113

Arabia 9
Arabia Felix (= Aden, *q.v.*) 10, 94, 104, 129
Arabs 179, 180
Arachosia 38, 40
Aragante 19
Arakan, R. 133
Aranyavāha 119
Arcadius 151, 154
Archebius 86
Archelaus of Carrha 142
Arch. Survey of India (1903–4) 169; (1912–13) 6
Arddhanārīshvara 146
Ariake 112
Ariana 71
arisi (*aruz* and ὄρυζα) 14
Aristobulus 105
Aristotle, *Hist. Anim.* 31, 116
Armenia 104
Armourers 53
Arrian, *Exped. Alex.* 34, 35; *Indika* 44, 49, 105
Arsakes 87
Arsinoe (Suez) 17, 89
Artabanus 75
Artaxerxes Mnemon 26
Artemidorus 86
Artha Śāstra 62, 67, 68
Arthur, king 159
Artizans 53
Aryans 2, 27, 31
Asia 19, 20, 161
Asia Minor 159
Aśoka 28, 39, 44, 58 ff., 68, 70, 79, 82, 162
Aśoka's Edicts 60, 62, 63; pillars 64
Asopus 27
Assam 27
Assurbanipal 2
Assyria 15
Assyrians 14, 16
Assyrian sculptures 31
Ἄστομοι 66
Asura Maya (= Ahura Mazda) 68
Aśvamedha 81
Aśvins, the (*Nāsatyā*) 2
Atharva Veda, 15
Athenaeus 48, 93
Athene 76
Athenodorus 129
Athens 88, 108
Augustus 101, 103 ff., 153
Aulus Gellius, *Noct. Att.* 29
Auranoboas (*or* Tyrannoboas) (?Aranyavāha *or* Mālvan) 119
Aurelian 154
aureus, Roman 150, 164, 166
Avidius Cassius 128
Ayodhya 43
Azes (I and II) 83, 86
Azilises 86

Bab-el-Mandeb 94
Babel 16
Bāberu (Babylon) 4
Babylon 1, 3, 4, 7, 12, 14 ff., 36, 155
Babylon, plague at 129
Babylonian marshes 6
Bacchus 60, 62
Bagdad 179
Bahrein Islands 6
Baktra (= Bākhtri = Bakhdhi = Balkh) 1, 2, 9, 16, 69, 88, 115, 160
Baktria 28, 83 ff., 108 148
Baktrian architecture 162
Baktrian Greeks 161 ff.
Baktrian kings 171
Bālaśrī 85
Balkh, *see* Baktra
Balsamodendron 125 126
Baluchistān 83, 126
Bankot 119
baobab tree 14
Barābar, caves at 68
Barake 111, 120
Barbarikon 35, 114, 124, 125
Bardesanes 142, 145, 174
Barhut 165
Barlaam and Josaphat (*see* St John of Damascus) 142
Barnett, L. D. 87; *Antiquities of India* 15, 61, 167, 172
Barygaza 3, 47, 95, 107, 108, 112, 113, 116, 124, 126, 131, 136, 170
Barzuyeh 179
Bassein 133
Baths of Caracalla 168
bdellium 125
Beal, S., *Life of Hiuen Tsiang* 143
Beās, R. 42, 43
Behistūn Inscriptions, the 17, 29
Benākaṭakā 162
Benfey, T., *Indien* 11; *Pañcha Tantra* 179
Bengal 122; Bay of 132
Berbera 92
Berenike 90, 91, 99, 111
Berosus 7

beryl (βήρυλλος from *vaiḍūrya*) 101, 120
Besatae 123
Besnagar 162
Besynga (*or* Bassein) 133
Bhagavad Gītā 178
Bharata, *Nāṭya Śāstra* 169
Bharukaccha 5
Bhavabhūti 170
Bhil races, the 22
Bhotān 27, 65
Bhoja, Narapati, *Yuktikalpataru* 139
Bhṛighu-Kaccha 116
Bhūmaka 87, 118
Bidpai (*or* Pilpay) 179
Bindusāra 39
Birdwood, Sir G. 126
Bisadae (*Besatae*) 147
blackwood 114
Bloch, *Ann. Report, Arch. Surv. Ind.* 169
Boghazköi, 3
Bolān Pass, the 83
Bolor Mts. 115
Bombay 6, 119; Prince of Wales Museum 6
Bombay Gazetteer 162
bos Lucas 13
Brachmanae 142
Brahmā 141
Brāhmaṇa (caste) 50 ff.
Brahmins 50 ff., 60 ff., 141, 147, 157, 160
Brahminism 79
Brāhmī-script, the 14
Brindisium 29
Broach 14, 116, 117, 119, 120
Buddha (*see also* Gautama) 11, 32, 157, 165
Buddha's tooth 149
Buddhism 23, 39, 58, 62, 78, 108, 138, 153, 157, 162, 168, 175
Buddhism, Hīnayāna 168
Buddhist architecture 28
Buddhist art 167
Buddhist ascetics 59
Buddhist Canon, the 60
Buddhist caves 85
Buddhist monasteries 143, 165
Buddhists 141 ff., 179
Bühler, J. G., *Origin of the Brāhma Alphabet* 4; *Indian Studies* 15
Bukephala (Jihlam) 34
Bunbury, *Hist. Anc. Geog.* 17, 69, 92, 94, 128
Bundelkhand 81
Burgess, J. 164; *Elephanta* 146
Burnet, *Early Greek Philosophy* 158
Byzantium (? Vizādrcg) 119

Cadiz 98
Caldwell, R. 122; *Dravidian Grammar* 14
Caligula 153
Camboja, Cape 132, 133
Cana 110
Canary Isles 99
Caracalla 153
Carinus 154
Carus 154
Caspian Gates, the 1, 9
Caspian Sea 1, 9
Catholic ceremonies 178
Celts 159
Ceylon 4, 5, 8, 9, 12, 72, 93, 104, 106, 109, 111, 147 ff.
Ceylon in the Classics 152
Chaldaea 7
Chaldaeans 6
Chālukyas 167
Champā 5, 132
Chāṇakya 37, 38, 54
Chaṇḍāla (*or* Pariah) 58
Chāndogya Upanishad 156
Chandragupta (= Sandrakottus, *q.v.*) 37 ff., 49 ff., 67, 80, 91, 161
Charaka 172
Charax 115
Chares, of Mitylene 100
Charibael (*Kariba-Il*) 113
Charition 139
Chastana 117
Chaucer, *Knight's Tale* 69; *Pardoner's Tale* 180
China 8, 9, 101, 131, 148 ff.
Chinese 66, 115, 116
Chitor 80
Chola Maṇḍalam or Chola-coast (= Coromandel) 122
Choromandae 66
Christianity 138, 175, 176
Chronicles II 10, 13
cinnamon 14, 30, 122, 125
Civil Service 55, 56
Claudius (41–54 A.D.) 106, 109, 113, 153
Claudius (268–270 A.D.) 154
Clement 138, 141, 142, 174
Cleopatra 97, 100

Clouston, *Originals and Analogues* 180
Cochin 121
Cochin lagoon, the 111
Code of Manu 138
coins 72 ff., 77, 78, 83 ff., 103, 150, 162, 164, 166, 167
Commodus 153
Constantine I 154
Constantine II 154
Constantinople 69, 88, 116, 152
Constantius 154
Coomaraswamy, A. K., *Arts and Crafts of India and Ceylon* 9
Corinthian pillars 168
Coromandel 122
Cos 115
costus (*kushṭha = kut-lākḍī*) 114, 124
courtezans 67
Cowell, E. B. 4
Cranganore 111, 120
Cunningham, A. 33; *Coins of Ancient India* 18; *Numismatic Chronicle* 73
Curtius, Quintus 33, 46
Curzon, Lord, *Persia* 68
Cyclops 66
Cyrus the Great 27
Cyzicus 96

Dabhai 42
Dafār 125
Dakshiṇāpatha (*see* Deccan) 118
Damascus 128, 179, 180
Damirike 110, 120
Dan 7
Dandamis (Damadamis) 143
Danube 66
Dardistān 18, 24, 102
Dards 66
Darius 16 ff., 27, 32, 89, 155; Palace of, at Persepolis 68
Darius (III) Codomannus 31
Dasyus, the 27
Dattamitra (*Demetria*) 162
Daulatabad 119
David, king of Judah 10
Davids, Rhys 5; *Buddhist Birth Stories* 12
De Abstinentia 143
Decameron 179
Deccan (*Dakkhinābada*), δάχανος (*see Dakshiṇāpatha*) 118
Deccan, North 84
Decian persecution 176
Decius 154
Dēimachus 39, 41
Deipnosophisies 94
De Lesseps 90
Delhi 52
Demetria (Arachosia) 72
Demetria (Sind) 72
Demetrius 72 ff., 78, 83, 85, 100, 115, 162
devas 145
Devgad 119
Dhābol 119
Dharma 29, 54, 80
Dikaios 31
Dīnāra, denarius 167
Dio Chrysostom 140
Diocletian 154
Diodorus Siculus 8
Diodotus (I and II) 70, 85
Diogenes 157
Diomedes 77, 86
Dion Cassius 107
Dionysius 39, 41, 92, 95
Dioskuri 74, 77
Dittenberger, W., *Orientis Graeci Inscriptiones Selectae* 92, 95
Doāb, the 44
Domitian 153
Dosarene (*Darśana*) 123
double-daric of Darius Codomannus 31
drachma 59, 150
dramma (mod. *dām*), δραχμή 167
Dravidians 19
drugs 102, 120, 124
"dumb Mlecchas" 47, 121
Duncker, M., *Gesch. des Alt.* 22
Dushyanta Rāja 47
Dutt, U. C., *Materia Medica of the Hindus* 126

Eagle (katreus) 108
ebony 113
Edfū, ruins at 99
Edom 10
Egypt 2, 9, 95, 101, 158, 161
Egyptians 158
Ekbatana 48, 115, 128
Elagabalus, Emperor 143
Elath 10
Eleazar 113
eleph, ox 13
ἐλεφαντ- (*root*) 13
Elephanta 146
Elephants 49, 52, 55, 91, 93
Eleusinian mysteries 146

Elysium of Yama, the 156
Emetreus 69
Emperors of the East 154
Encyclopaedia Britannica 15, 126
Ency. of Religion and Ethics 180
'Ενωτοκοῖται (= *karṇaprāvaraṇa*) 65
Epander 86
Eratosthenes 40, 92, 93, 95, 105
Ersch and Grüber's *Encyclopaedia* 11
Essenes, the 176
"Etesian" winds 109
Ethiopia 149; palace of 151
Ethiopians 18, 19
Eudaemon (= Aden, *q.v.*) 94
Eudamus 36, 71
Eudoxus 18, 96 ff., 100, 138
Euergetes II 97, 100
Eukratides 72 ff., 83, 85
Eumenes 36
Euphrates, R. 1, 2, 42, 113, 127, 129
Euripides 170
Eusebius 141
Euthydemeia 70
Euthydemus I 70 ff., 76, 77, 85
Euthydemus II 86
Euxine, the 1, 9
Ezekiel 6, 20
Ezion Geber (= Aelana, *q.v.*) 10, 90

Fabulous races 65, 66
Fa-Hian 58, 60
fakirs 60
Falconer, Keith, *Bidpai* 179
Fausböll 25
Firmicus Maternus 174
Fleet, Dr J. F. 87, 172
Flood, the 15
frankincense 113, 124

Galba 153
Gallienus 154
Gallus 154
Gandarii, the 19
Gandhāra 16, 17, 28, 32, 42, 77, 165, 167
Gandhāra pottery 171
Gandhāra sculptures 84, 163, 167, 168
Ganges 30, 38, 41 ff., 53, 64, 78, 105, 122, 123, 126, 131 ff., 161
Gangetic Gulf, the 132
Ganjām, R. 132
Garbha-Rakshaṇa 61
Gardafui, Cape 97, 110
Gardner, P., *Cat. of Greek and Indo-Scythic Coins in B.M.* 72, 76 ff., 85, 164
Gārgī Saṃhitā 81, 173
Garuḍa pillar 162
Garuḍa, the vulture of Vishṇu 65
Gautama (*see also* Buddha) 22, 23, 58, 59, 82, 142, 157, 178
Gaza 128, 129
Gazetteer of the Bombay Presidency 126
Gedrosia 38
gems 114
Genesis 11
Geography of Ravenna 120
Γεωργοί (*Husbandmen*) 51
Gerrha, 6
Gesta Romanorum 179
Gibbon, E., *Decline and Fall of the Roman Empire* 102
Gibraltar 98
Glaser, *Skizze der Geog. Arab.* 11
Gnosticism 138, 177
Goa 119
Golden Chersonese, the 5, 11, 43, 120, 133
Goldstücker, T., *Pāṇini, his place in Sanskrit Literature* 32
Gollas 148
Gondophares 83, 87
Gordians, the 154
Goths 151, 155
Gray, L. H. 180
Greece 13
Greek amphitheatre 169
"Greek curtain" 169, 170
Greek drama 169
Greek sculptors 165
Greek kings of Baktria, Sāgala, and the Panjāb 69 ff., 85, 86
Greeks 82, 83
Gregory XIII 142
Grenfell and Hunt, *Oxyrhynchus Papyri* 139
Gṛihya Sūtras 61
Grundriss der Ind.-Ar. Philologie 31
Gujarat (Ariake) 118, 139
Gulliver's Travels 30
Gupta monarchs 166; period 168
Gymnosophists 142

Hadrian 153
Halikarnassus 21
Hamilton, Capt., *New Account of the East Indies* 124

Hamīrpur 82
Hastināpura 42, 43
Hastings, J., *Dictionary of the Bible* 11; *Dict. Religion and Ethics* 169
Havilah 11
Hector 140, 170
Hecuba 170
Hekataeus (of Miletus) 16, 19, 20, 25, 26, 41, 66; *Periegesis* 19
Hekatompylus 1, 115, 128
Helen of Troy 140
Heliodorus 162
Heliogabalus 153
Heliokles 73, 76, 77, 85
Hellenic influence 170, 172
Hellenism 161, 162
Helmand 83
Herakles 60, 61, 141
Heraklitus 176
Hercules, temple of, at Erythrae 24
Herdsmen 51, 52
Hermaeus 84, 86
Hermes 139
Herodotus 3, 7, 16 ff., 30, 44, 89, 158
Heroopolite Gulf 89
Hēsidrus, the 64
Himālayas 25, 108
Hīnayāna Buddhism 168
Hindu (*and variants*) 20
Hinduism 162
Hindu Kush 8, 21, 38, 75, 125, 161
Hindus 58, 60
Hippalus 109 ff., 120
Hippokleides 25
Hippokrates 172
Hippostratus 86
Hippuri (Kudremale) 150
Hira 115
Hiram, king of Tyre 10
Hirth, F., *China and the Roman Orient* 111, 115, 130
Hiuen Tsiang 51, 59, 68, 118, 143, 148, 149
Hiuen Tsiang, Life of (trans. by S. Beal) 149
Homer 18, 140, 156, 169 ff.; *Iliad* 140, 172; *Odyssey* 18
Homerites 113
Honorius 151, 152
Hopkins, E. W., *Great Epic of India* 68
Huan-ti 130
Huc, Abbé 178
Huc et Gabet, *Voyages* 179
Hultzsch, Dr 100, 139
Huns, White 148
Huvishka 87
Hydaspes, R. 34
Hyderabad 119
Hydreumata 90; Apollo 91; New 91
Hylobioi (*Vānaprastha*) 62, 176
Hyparkhus, R. (? Ganges) 30
Hyperboreans, the 25, 66
Hyphasis, R. 33, 64

Iamblichus 157
Ibn Jāfar Almansūr 179
Ichthyophagi 21
inchiver (ζιγγίβερις) 14
India, coast of 131
India and the Roman Empire 101–154
Indian Antiquary 164, 178
Indian buildings 168
Indian drama 169 ff.
Indian literature 169 ff.
Indian Ocean 19
indigo 114
Indo-Aryan village community 52
Indo-Parthian dynasty 84, 87
Indo-Parthians 163, 167
Indra 2, 61
Indrāgnidatta 162
Indus, R. 1, 2, 16, 18, 19, 30, 35, 41, 44, 53, 78, 114, 117
Intaphernes 25
intercourse between India and the West 155
Ionians 20 (*see Yavana, Yonakas*)
Ipsus, battle of 92
Irān 28
Iranian deities 165
Iranians 69, 163
Irrawady delta 133
Isaiah 3, 11, 20
Isidore of Charax, Σταθμοὶ Παρθικοί 128
Italy 98
ivory 5, 10, 120, 123

Jacobi, H., *De Horæ Originibus* 174
Jaigaḍ 119
Jaimini Bhārata 177
Jains 60, 157
jāmitra (διάμετρον) 174

Jamnā, R. 42, 53, 64
jangāla 122
Jātaka 4, 5, 7, 11, 12, 168, 179, 180
Java 131, 134, 138, 139
Javan 7
Jews 176
jewels 120
Jifātin Islands 91
Jihlam 34, 42
Job, Book of 11
John of Damascus, St 142
Josephus, *Ant. Jud.* 11
Journal of Philology 25, 180
Journal of the Royal Asiatic Society 68, 100, 107, 118, 121, 124, 151, 162, 163, 165, 166, 171, 172
Journal of the Royal Society of Arts 126
Jovian 154
Judaea 3, 10
Julian 154
Julius Caesar, *De Bello Gallico* 159
Justin 6, 37, 75, 76
Justinian 116
Justinus 151

Kābul 17, 77, 84
Kābul valley 83
Kaḍphises I (Kujūla) 84, 87, 107, 108, 164; II (Wima) 87, 109, 164
Kaenitae (? Kārwāḍ) 119
Kalanos 59, 108
Kalasi 78
Kālidāsa 47, 170, 172, 174; *Śakuntalā* 47
Kālīnadī 42
Kalinga 139
Kalinipaxa (? Kanyākubja *or* Kanauj) 42, 64, 65
Kalliaṭiae (? Kaliantiae) 19
Kalyān 119, 148
Kamara (*Khaberis emporium*) 122
Kampot (*or* Kang-Kao), R. 132
Kaṃsa 177
Kanarese dialect 140
Kanauj 42
Kane 113
Kang-Kao, R. 132
Kāṇheri 146
Kanishka 79, 84, 87, 109, 164, 165, 168, 171
Kanyākubja 42
Kāpiśa 72, 77
Kappadokia, 2
kara (taxes) 177
Karachi 124
Kārla caves 85, 162
Karmania 110
Karmanian Desert, the 1, 9, 16, 70
kārp̣p̣u (κάρπιον) 14, 30
Kārwāḍ 119
Karyanda 21, 158
Kashgar 69, 115
Kashmīr (Kāśyapa-mīra) 16, 114, 124
Kasii 115
Kaspapyrus 16, 19, 20
κασσίτερος (*kastīra*) 13
Kathaei, the 59
Kathiāwār, 59, 71
Kattigara (? Kian-chi) 133, 135, 136
Kausia 74
Kauṭilīya Artha Śāstra 41, 67, 68, 118
Kauṭilya (*or* Chāṇakya) 67, 68
Kāviri, R. 121, 122
Kaye, J. W. 172
Keith, A. B. 2; *Pythagoras and Transmigration* 156
Kennedy, J. 2, 177
Kerobothra (*or* Keralaputra) 120
khaḍga (καρτάζωον) 30
Khaibar, the 43
Khandahār 83
Kharōshṭhī script 28, 32, 72
Kian-chi (*and see* Kattigara) 136
Kings I 10, 13
Kirāṭa 27
Kirātāśin 65
Kirrhadii (= *Kirāta*) 65
Kleitarchus 60, 108
Kling (= India) 139
Koft (*and see* Koptos) 90
kolandia 122
Koniaki 93
koph (*kapi*) 11, 13
Koptos (= Koft, *q.v.*) 90, 91, 111
Kory, Cape 93, 131
Kosmas Indikopleustes 5, 92, 104, 124, 147 ff., 152; *Christian Topography* 104
Kottonara (*Kolatta-nadu, i.e.* Tellicherry) 112
Krishṇa 177
Kshaharāta clan 84
Kshaharāta princes 167
Kshattriya (caste) 50 ff.

Ktesias 8, 14, 16 ff., 29 ff.; 33, 66, 155; *Indika* 26; *Persika* 27
Ktesiphon 1, 115, 128
Kubjā 177
Kuhn's Zeitschrift 2
Kumārasambhava 174
Kumāri, Cape 122
Kumārī or Devī 122
Κυνάμολγοι 66
Kunaxa, battle of 26
Κυνοκέφαλοι (= *Śvamukha*) 66
Kushān kings 84, 87, 103, 163, 164
Kushāns 84, 101, 114, 161, 162, 165, 167

Laccadive islands (=*Laksha dvīpa*) 147
Lacôte, F., *Essai sur Guṇādhya et le Bṛihatkathā* 180
Ladāk 24
Lamaist ritual 178
Lassen 29 ff., 42; *Indische Altherthumskunde* 11, 17, 29, 123
Law, N. N., *The Ancient Hindu Polity* 68
Leipsius, *Denkmäler* 99
leṇa 162
Leo I 154; II 154
Leuke Kome 90, 129
Levant 115
Lévi, Sylvain, *Théâtre Indien* 169
Lhassa 178
Liaka Kusūlaka 83, 87
Libya, 19, 66
Lillie, A., *India in Primitive Christianity* 176
Lindner, *Die Iranische Flutsage* 15
Linnaean Society, Trans. of 126
Lixus, R. 98
Llamas 179
Lōeb Classical Library 142
Logos, doctrine of the 176
Lorinser, Dr, *Die Bhagavad Gītā* 178
Lucium 29
Lucretius 13
lycium (berberry) 114, 125
Lysias 86

McCrindle, J. W., *Ancient India* 8, 22, 23, 26, 66, 77, 142, 152, 157
Macdonell, A. A., *Hist. of Sansk. Lit.* 169; *Vedic Index* 15
Macrinus 153
Madeira 99
Madhyadeśa 82
Madhyamikā 80, 81, 117
Madras 102, 122
Madura 166
Maes (Titianus) 115
Maesolia (Masalia) 132
Magadha 33, 38, 80
Mahābhārata 23, 27, 68, 172, 178
Mahāpadma (*see* Xandrames) 33
Mahāparinibbāna Sutta 82
Mahāvaṃsa 4, 34, 35
Mahoshadha Jātaka 11
Μακρόβιοι 66
Malabar (Male) 110, 148
Malacca, Straits of 131
Malala, Johannes 152
Mālavikāgnimitra 81
Malay Peninsula 133
malobathrum 123, 125
Mālvan 119
Mālwā 117
Mambarus (? Nahapāna) 118
Manār, gulf of 150
Mandagora (? Bankot) 119
Mandanis 62
Mandeville, Sir John 26
Mangalore 120
Mangaroutha (Mangalore) 148
Manicheans, the 138
Manicheism 177
Manu 53, 57; code of 138
Marcellus, theatre of 109
Marcion 154
Marco Polo 149
Marcus Aurelius 127, 129, 153
Mardonius 27
Marinus of Tyre 130, 132
Marseilles 98
Marshall, Sir J. H. 163, 165, 171
Martichora 30
Marusthālī 21
Masalia 123
Massacre of the Innocents 177
Massagetae, the 22
Masulipatam district 132
Mathurā 80, 81, 83, 87, 177
Maues (= Moga = Moa?) 83, 86
Mauretania 98
Maurya Emperors 28, 39, 79, 81, 117, 160 ff.
Maurya Empire, the 29, 33 ff., 49 ff., 70, 161
Maximinus 154

Medicine, Greek and Indian 172
Mediterranean, the 4, 19, 88
Mediterranean ports 8
Megasthenes 22, 23, 26, 28, 33 ff., 39 ff., 49 ff., 67, 68, 93, 105, 109, 142, 174
Megisba, lake 153
Mekrān coast 6, 21; desert 35
Melizigara (? Jaigaḍ) 110, 119
Memnonian Susa 48
Menander 72, 76 ff., 82, 86, 114, 116, 117, 162, 171, 172
Merchant of Venice 180
Μηρός (Bacchus legend) 61
Meru, Mount 61
Mesopotamia 128
Metempsychosis (παλιγγενεσία) 156, 159, 177
Meyer, E. 2
Milinda (= Menander, *q.v.*) 77
Milinda Pañha 77 ff.; Siamese version of the 82
Milton 20
Minayef, Prof. 4
Minnagara (*Min-nagara*) 114
Mitanni, in Kappadokia 2
Mithradates 73
Mitra 2
Mitra, Rajendralāl 139
Moabite Stone, the 15
Mocha (= Muza, *q.v.*) 94
Moga, *see* Maues
Moghal Empire 92
Mommsen, Th., *Provinces of the Roman Empire* 103
Mon. Ancyranum 107
Mongolian hillmen 123
Mongolians 65
Μονόμματοι (= *Ekāksha*) 66
Moon, temple of the, at Mugheir 3
Morin, Jean, *Dessin des Animaux en Grèce* 9
Moscha 113
Moses, bishop of Adule 147
Mṛicchakaṭikā 169
Mudrā Rākshasa 46, 47
Mugheir 3
Mukerji, R., *Indian Shipping* 5, 121, 139
Mukti (Emancipation) 175
Müller, Carl, *Frag. Hist. Graec. Min.* 39
Müller, Max 26; *Physical Religion* 2; *Selected Essays* 142
muslin 100, 117, 123
Muza (= Mocha) 94, 95, 112
Muziris (? *Muyiri-kotta*) (= Cranganore), Malabar coast, 108, 111, 120, 121
Myos Hormos (Mussel Harbour) 91, 104, 106, 111
Myrrh 125, 126

Nahapāna 84, 87
Naksh-i-Rastam inscriptions 17
Nālandā monastery 143
NANAIA (Anaitis, the goddess) 164
Nanda 177
Nanda Rāja (? Xandrames) 33
Nandrus 37
Nārada 178
nard (citronella) 114
Nardostachys Jatamansi 126
Narmadā, R. 116, 117
Nāsatyā (the Aśvins) 2
Nāsik 118; caves 85, 162
Nations of India 147
Naukratis 89
Naustathmos (Alexander's Haven) 35
Nearchus 35, 55, 105
Nebuchadnezzar I 3; II 7
Negrais, Cape 132
Nelkynda (? *Nil-kantha*) 108, 111, 120, 121, 130
Neo-platonism 138, 141, 142, 175
Neo-platonists 175
Neo-Sassanian Empire 151
Nepal 65, 115
Nero 104, 127, 153
Nerva 153
Nestorian Church 148, 177
Nicolaus of Damascus 108
Nikaea 34
Nikias 86
Nile, the 19, 30, 44, 88 ff.
Nineveh 1, 7
Noah 5
Nubia 91
Numerian 154
Nushirvan, king of Persia 179

Okēlis 111, 112
Ὠκύποδες (= Μονόσκελοι = Μονόκωλοι) 66
Oldenburg, H. 2
olibanum (al-luban) 125
Oman, coast of 12
Ommana 113
Onesikritus 62, 105
Ophir 1, 10 ff., 17

Opiae, the 19
Oppert, G., *Trade with Ancient India* 126
Orathra (Surāshṭra) 148
Origen 138, 177
Orissa 123
Orosius 74
Orphic schools 156
Orthagnes 87
ὄρυζα 14
Ostasiatische Zeitschrift 9
Othello 26
Otho 153
'Ωτόκλινοι 65
Overseers ('Επίσκοποι) 54
Oxus, R. 1, 9, 69, 70, 74, 75, 161
Oxydrakae, the 61
Oxyrhynchus 139
Oxyrhynchus Papyri 139
Ozene (= Ujjain) 117

Padaei, the (? Bhīls) 22
Padiyūr 101
pāduka 168
Pahlava tribes 83
Paitāmaha Siddhānta 173
Paithān 119
Pakhtū (Pashtū *or* Pathāns) 17
Pakhtū district 21
Pakores 87
Paktyike 16, 17
Palaesimundus (? *Palaisimanta*) 152
Palaipatmai (? Dhābol *or* Pāripatana) 119
Palibothra 65
Palmyra 2, 128, 129
Palura 131, 132
Pamirs, the 71
Pan 141
Pañcha Tantra 179
Pañchāla country 81
panchāyats 56, 59, 67
Pandion 107
Πανδορή 66
Pāṇḍya (Pandion) kings of Madurā 107, 120
Pāṇḍyas 167
Panemus 163
Pāṇini 32, 158
Panjāb, the 1, 7, 21, 24, 34, 63, 76, 108, 114, 160, 161, 165, 167, 171
Pantaenus 141
Pantaleon 86
Pariahs 58
Pāripatana 119
Paropamisus 71
Parthenon 170
Parthia 69, 70, 89, 128
Parthians 83, 129, 130
Paruparaesanna (Paropamisus) 17
Paśchādaṅgulaja 27, 66
Patala (Patalene) (= Bahmanābād) 34, 35
Pātala (Potana) 94, 110, 114
Pāṭaliputra 38, 40, 41 ff., 68, 79, 80, 93, 161
Patañjali 81, 175
Pātika 83, 87, 163
Pativedakā 51
Patrokles 93
Pattalene 71
Paul of Alexandria 173, 176
Pauliśa Siddhānta 173
Pausanias 31
Pax Romana 101
Pegu 133
Peithon 36
pepper 102, 112, 120, 147, 151
Periplus Maris Erythraei 3, 17, 20, 47, 65, 94, 95, 106, 110, 112, 113, 116, 118, 130, 132 ff., 136, 147, 152, 170
Persepolis 68
Persepolis inscriptions, the 17
Persia 15, 148, 149, 178
Persian Gulf 1, 6, 12, 17, 35, 113
Persian period, the 16 ff.
Peshāwar 161, 165, 171
Petra 90, 115, 128, 129
'petri' (*patra*, leaves) 123
Peukelaotis (*Pushkalāvatī*) 42, 64
Peukelaus 86
Peutinger Tables 120, 121
Pharaoh Necho 89
Philip 154
Philip, satrap of Parthia 35
Philo 176
Philosophers 51
Philostratus 107, 146
Philoxenus 86
Phison, the (of Genesis) 148
Phoenicians 6, 7, 12
Photius 26, 29, 40; *Bibliotheke* 31
Pillay, *The Tamils eighteen hundred years ago* 47, 121
Pilpay (*or* Bidpai) 179
pipali (πέπερι) 14
Plato 61, 157; *Laws* 158; *Republic* 157
Plato, Baktrian king 86

Plautus, *Mercator* 139
Pliny 5, 20, 24, 39 ff., 66, 92, 102, 104, 105, 110, 112, 115, 124, 126, 150, 152
Plutarch 77, 82, 170; *Vit. Alex.* 33, 141; *Sertorius* 99
πνευματικοί 177
Poduca (Puducheri *or* Pondicherry) 122
Polybius 74, 92
Pompeii 105
Poppoea 104
Porphyry 141, 142, 174
Port Said 94
Port Sudan 92
Portuguese 14
Porus (= Paurava) 36, 40, 92, 107
Poseidonius 96
Potana (= Pātala, *q.v.*) 94
Prākrit 171
Prasii, the 33
Prasii, country of the 152
Prayāga 42, 43, 51, 56, 65
Priam 140, 169
Priaulx, O. de B., *Indian Travel* 107, 140; *Indian Embassies to Rome* 107, 130, 140; *Life of Apollonius of Tyana* 140
Probus 154
Psalms, Book of 11
Pseudo-Kallisthenes 147, 148
ψυχικοί 177
Ptolemais Epitherōn (Ptolemais of the Hunts) 91, 92
Ptolemies, the 88–100
Ptolemy Auletes 100
Ptolemy Epiphanes 100
Ptolemy Euergetes I 92, 100; II 100
Ptolemy Lathyrus 97
Ptolemy Philadelphus 18, 19, 39, 48, 65, 71, 89, 90 ff., 100
Ptolemy Philometor 100
Ptolemy Philopator 94, 100
Ptolemy Soter I 100; II 94, 100
Ptolemy (Claudius Ptolemaeus), *Guide to Geography* 90, 106, 115, 130 ff.
puchuk 124
Puṃ-Savana 61
"Punt, the land of" 10
Purāṇic legends 160
Pushyamitra 81
Pygmies (Τρισπίθαμοι) 27, 65, 66
Pyrrhus 92
Pythagoras 61
Pythagorean philosophy 156, 175; schools 156; "tabus" 157

Rachia (*Rājā*) 152
Rājagṛiha 43
Rājavula 83, 87
Rājputāna 81
Rājputāna desert, the 21
Rāmāyaṇa 22, 43, 141, 172
Rāmgarh, Greek amphitheatre at 169
Ran of Kacch 116
Rapson, E. J., *Coins of the Āndhras* 162; *Indian Coins* 167
Ras abn Somer, bay of 91
Rawlinson, H. G., *Baktria* 73
Ray, P. C. 178
Red Sea 1, 9, 10, 88, 90
Reinaud, *Relations de l'Empire Romain avec l'Asie Oriental* 130
relic-worship 141, 176
Rhinokolura (= El Arish) 90, 129
Rhodopha (? Dabhai) 42, 64
Ridge, the (Delhi) 52
Ṛig Veda, 3, 4, 15, 156, 176
"*Romaka*" (= Alexandria) 173
Romakākhyā prakīrtitā 173
Romaka Siddhānta 173
Romance History of Alexander 147
Roman Emperors 153, 163, 164
Roman Empire 163
Rome 101, 173
Roth, *Festgruss* 15
Rouse, W. H. D. 4
Royal City, the 44
Royal Councillors 54
Royal Road (Maurya domains) 29, 42, 64
Royal Road (Persia) 43
Royal Tombs of the Persian Kings 68
Ruanvelli, the great tope of 34

Sabaites 113
Sada 132
Sāgala (? Siālkot) 71, 79, 161, 162, 171
St Anthony 176
St Bartholomew 141
St Chrysostom, *Orations* 169
St Jerome 138
St John of Damascus, *Barlaam and Josaphat* 19, 142, 180
St Josaphat 142

St Mark 126
St Martin, *Étude sur la Géog. Grecque* 64
St Matthew 141
Śaka (Sakae) tribe 75, 77, 82 ff., 163
Śaka dynasties 83, 86, 103, 161, 167
Śaka era 87
Sakastene (= Seistān) 83
Sāketa 80, 81
Śakti rites 61
Śakuntalā 47
ΣΑΛΗΝΗ 165
Sammurammat 8
Samos 109
Samudra Gupta 166
Sānchi 165
Sandales, *see* Sandanes
Sandalwood 113
Sandanes (*Sundara Śātakarṇi*) 119, 143, 146
Sandbares 87
Sandrakottus (= Chandragupta, *q.v.*) 24, 28, 29, 37
saṅgāra (catamarans) 122
Sāṅkhya system 177
San letter, the 164
Sanskrit literature 179
Sapphara Metropolis 125
sapphire, a gigantic 149
Saraganus, the elder 119
Sarikol, Stone Tower of 69, 115
Sarmanes (*see also Śramaṇa*) 60, 62, 142
Sassanian dynasty 150
Sassanian Empire 166
Śatapatha Brāhmaṇa 15
Satī 59
Saussurea lappa 114, 124
Sayce, A. H. 2, 3; *Hibbert Lectures* 3; *Science of Language* 179
Schliemann, H., *Ilios* 8
Schwanbeck 23, 33, 40, 44, 49, 50
Seistān (= Sakastene) 83
Seleukids 29, 100
Seleukus I 100; II (*Kallinikus*) 100; III (*Soter*) 100; IV (*Philopator*) 100
Seleukus Nikator 38, 39, 49, 64, 91, 93
Semiramis 8, 27, 35
Semitic Empires of W. Asia 16
Semitic races 160
Sen, K. A. 126
Sennacherib 6, 114
Septimius Severus 151, 153
Septuagint, the 11
Seres 43, 79, 152
Sertorius 99
Sesikrienae (? Vengurla) 119
Sesostris 89
Sewell, R., *Roman Coins found in India* 103, 121, 151
Shalmaneser III 3
Sheba 11
shen habbin (*ibhadanta*), ivory 11
shipwrights 53
Siam, Gulf of 132, 133
Sibae, the 61
Sibor (Simylla *or* Chaul) 148
Siddhāntas, five 173
Sidon, 2, 128
Sieladiba (*Sinhala dvīpa*) 149
Sigertis 71
Sigerus 110
Śīlāditya 51
"silent barter" 124, 152
silk 101, 115, 123, 128
Silver Country 132, 134
Sind 36, 114
Sindhava 20
Sindhu, "Indian cotton" 2
Sindhu, R. 81
Sinhalese merchants 124
Sinhalese (*or* Lion people) 5, 149, 153
Sinus Aelaniticus 10
Sītā 141
Śiva 61, 141, 146
Skeat, W. W., *Oxford Chaucer* 180
Skiapodes, the 19, 26, 27, 66
Skōlēx 30
Skylax of Karyanda 16 ff., 24, 30, 65, 96, 111, 155, 158
Skythians 161, 163
Slavery 58
Smith, V. A. 107, 118; *Early History of India* 37, 47, 71, 83, 121; *Graeco-Roman Influence on Ancient Indian Civilization* 172
Soanus, R. 81
Śodāsa 83, 87
Sogdiana 75
Sokotra 94, 148
Sokotra (Dioscorida = *Sukhādhāra-dvīpa*)
Solinus 40
Solomon 11, 13

Soma juice, 58
Somali coast, the 104
Somaliland 9
Son, R. 44, 45
Sona, R. (*or* Hiraṇyabāhu) 24
Sonaparānta (Aurea Regio) 133
Sopāra 119
Σωφάρα (Ophir in the Septuagint) 11
Sophir, Coptic term for Southern India 11
Sophokles 170; *Antigone* 171
Sophon 99
Soptama (*Su-patana*) 122
Spalirises 87
spices 102, 104, 120, 125, 126
Spikenard (*Nardostachys Jatamansi*) 120, 126
Spooner, D. B. 68
Śramaṇa (*or* Buddhists, *q.v.*) 141, 160
Sramanaioi 176
stactē 126
Statīra, stater 167
Stein, A., *Ancient Geography of Kaśmīr* 17; *Zoroastrian Deities on Indo-Scythian Coins* 164
Stobaeus, *Physica* 144
"Stone Tower" of Sarikol 115
Storax (Benzoin) 126
Strabo 6, 8, 9, 22 ff., 39 ff., 58 ff., 66, 77 ff., 89 ff., 104 ff., 115, 129, 133, 137
Strato 76, 77, 86
Stromata, ed. Dindorf 141
Στρουθόποδες 66
stūpa (or *tope*) 141, 165
Styracaceae 126
Subhāgasena 92
Sudan 92
Śūdra (caste) 50 ff.
Suez (= Arsinoe, *q.v.*) 1, 2, 12, 17, 18, 89, 111
Sulla 104
Sumatra 131, 148
Sumer 16
Śunga kings 80
Suppāra 5, 11
Surāshṭra (= Kathiāwār and Surāt districts) 71
Surāt 117
Sūryya Siddhāntas 173
Susa 26, 28
Sutlej, R. 42
Suvarṇabhūmi 5, 133
Śvetadvīpa 178
Swiss Guards 48
Syagrus, Cape (Ras Fārtak) 110, 113
Syburtius 40
Syrastrene (*Surāshṭra*) 117
Syria 89, 101
Syrian art 167
Syrian Empire 93

Tacitus 154
tāḍī 30
Takshasilā (*see* Taxila) 162
Tāmluk 42
Tāmralipti 5, 123
Tanjore 9
Tapropane (*Tāmraparṇī*) 149
Tarn, W. W. "Hellenism in Baktria" 73
Tarshish 7
Tawney, C. H. 25, 81, 180
Taxila 28, 29, 42, 43, 56, 59, 63, 83, 87; inscription 163
teak 113
Telang, K. T., trans. of *Bhagavad Gītā* 178
Telephus 86
Tellicherry 112
Temala (*or* Tamala) 132
temples, Assyrian 114; Chaldean 114; rock 146
Tennant, Emerson, *Ceylon* 153
Ter (Tāgara) 119
Terebinthus 138, 142
Thapsacus 9
Thebaid, the 176
Theodosius I 154; II 154
Theophrastus, *History of Plants* 124
Therapeutae 176
Thermopylae 27
Thomas, the apostle 84
Thrace 156
Thracians 159
Three Caskets, story of the 180
"three *guṇas*" 177
"three qualities" 177
thuki-im (*tokei*) 11
Tiastanes 117
Tiberius 103, 153
tigers 109
Tigris, R. 128
Tinavelly 14
Tissa Wēwa 153
Titus 153
Togarum (? Devgaḍ) 119

Tokosanna, R. 133
tortoise-shell 120
Toy Cart 169 ff.
τραχηλίζοντες 110
Trajan 109, 127, 129, 140, 153, 163, 164
Trans-Gangetic India 133
Trial by Ordeal 144
trikoṇa (τρίγωνος) 174
Trimurti, shrine of the 146
Turkestan 148
Tykta 63
Tyrannoboas, *see* Auranoboas
Tyre, 2, 7, 10, 89, 115, 128, 129

Ucchaṅga Jātaka 25
Ujjain 56, 117, 173
ὑλικοί 177
Ummaga Jātaka 12
uplet 124
"Ur of the Chaldees" 3
Uttara-kuru (= Attakorae) 25, 66

Vāch 176
vaiḍūrya (βήρυλλος) 14
Vaiśya (caste) 50 ff.
Valens 154
Valerian 154
Vallabhas of Gujarat 177
Vānaprastha 62
Vaniyambāḍi 101
Varāhamihira 173, 174; *Bṛihat Saṃhitā* 173; *Hora Jñāna* 174; *Pañcha Siddhāntikā* 173
Varuṇa 2
Vasco da Gama 99, 102
Vāśishṭha Siddhānta 173
Vāsudeva 87
Vedabbha Jātaka 180
Vedas, the 156
Veddas 124
Vedic gods 2
Vengi (*i.e.* Kalinga) dialect 139
Vengurla 119
Vergil, *Georgics* 116
Vespasian 103, 153
vidūshaka (parasite) 169
Vijaya, prince, of Bengal 4
Vikings 121
Vikramāditya era 87
Vilivāyakura II 118
Vishṇu 15
Vishṇu Purāṇa 177
viṭa (pimp) 169
Vitellius 153
Vizādrog 119
Vonones 83, 87
Von Schröder, L., *Indiens Lit. und Cultur* 169, 174; *Pythagoras und die Inder* 158

Watts, G., *Commercial Products of India* 126
Weber, A. 177, 178; *Indian Literature* 172; *Indische Studien* 178; *Sanskrit Literature* 169
White Huns 148
Wilson, H. H., *Ariana Antiqua* 17
Wima Kadphises 87
Winckler, H. 2
Windisch, E., *Greek Influence on Indian Drama* 169

Xandrames (Mahāpadma) 33
Xerxes 27, 68

Yavana, Yavanī, 31, 38, 71, 81 ff., 117, 121, 158, 169, 173
Yavanapura (= Alexandria) 173
Yavanikā 169
Yoga doctrine of Patañjali 175
Yogis 60
Yonakas, "Yonas" 79
Yueh-chi 75, 82, 84
Yule, H. 132; *Cathay and the way Thither* 131; *Marco Polo* 126

Zaba (Zabæ) 132, 133
Zamorin, of Calicut 102
Zarathustrian influence 177
Zarmanochegas (*Śramaṇāchārya*), Buddhist monk 107
Zend Avesta 72
Zeugma 128
Zeus Ombrios 61
Zodiac, signs of the 173
Zoilus 86